If you started with THE CIRCLE SERIES . . .

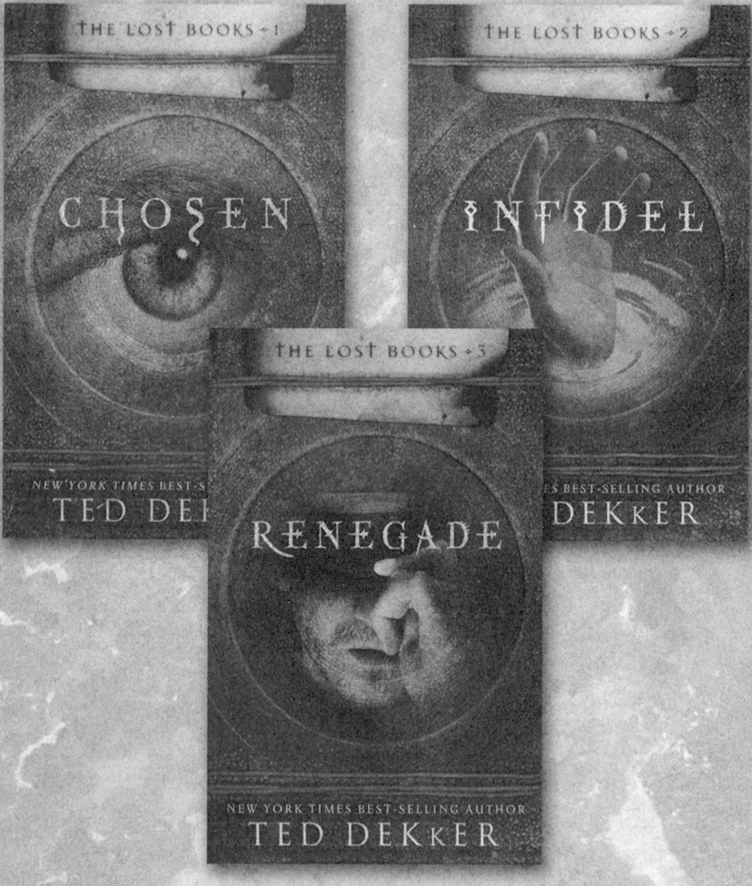
THE LOST BOOKS • 1
CHOSEN
THE LOST BOOKS • 2
INFIDEL
THE LOST BOOKS • 3
RENEGADE
NEW YORK TIMES BEST-SELLING AUTHOR
TED DEKKER

The Lost Books

YOU ONLY KNOW PART OF THE STORY

The Lost Books Graphic Novels

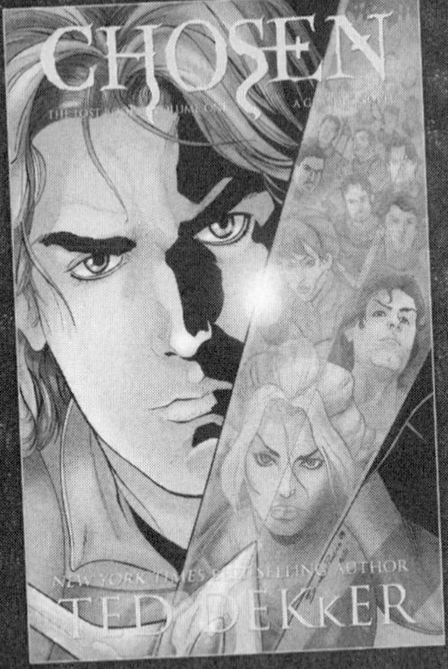
CHOSEN
NEW YORK TIMES BEST-SELLING AUTHOR
TED DEKKER

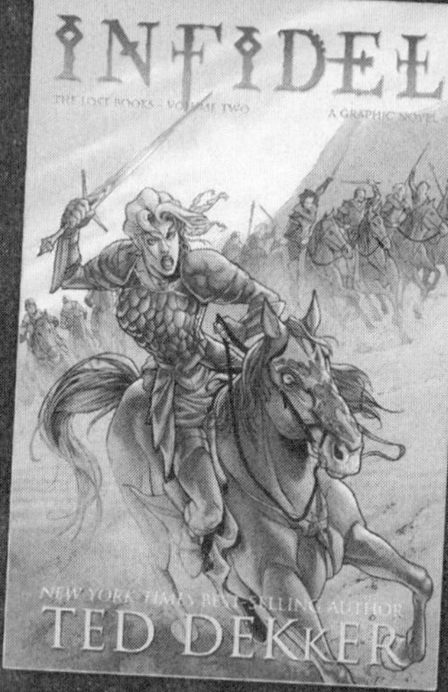
INFIDEL
THE LOST BOOKS - VOLUME TWO
A GRAPHIC NOVEL
NEW YORK TIMES BEST-SELLING AUTHOR
TED DEKKER

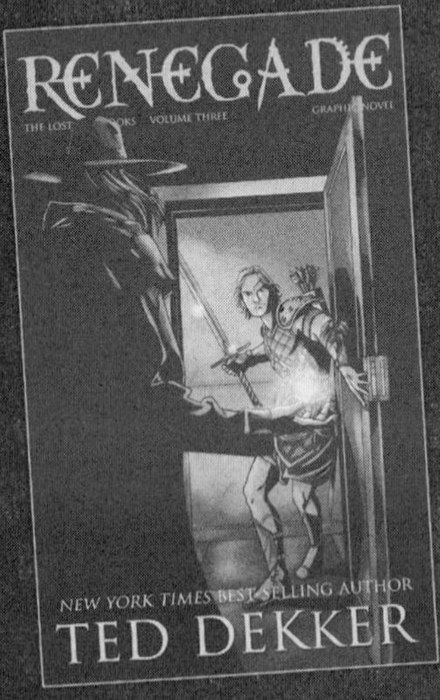
RENEGADE
VOLUME THREE
NEW YORK TIMES BEST-SELLING AUTHOR
TED DEKKER

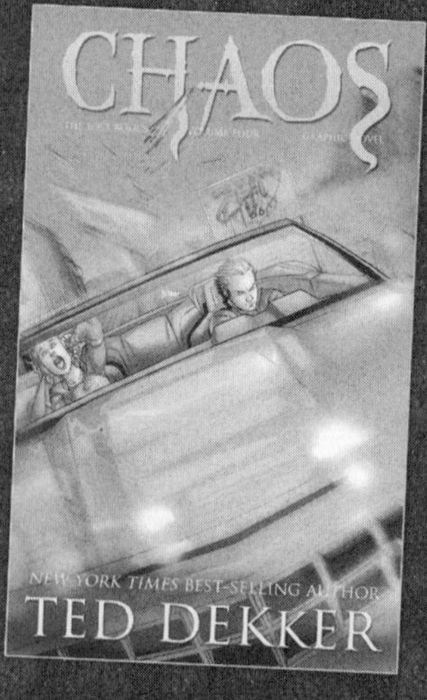
CHAOS
NEW YORK TIMES BEST-SELLING AUTHOR
TED DEKKER

Available Now

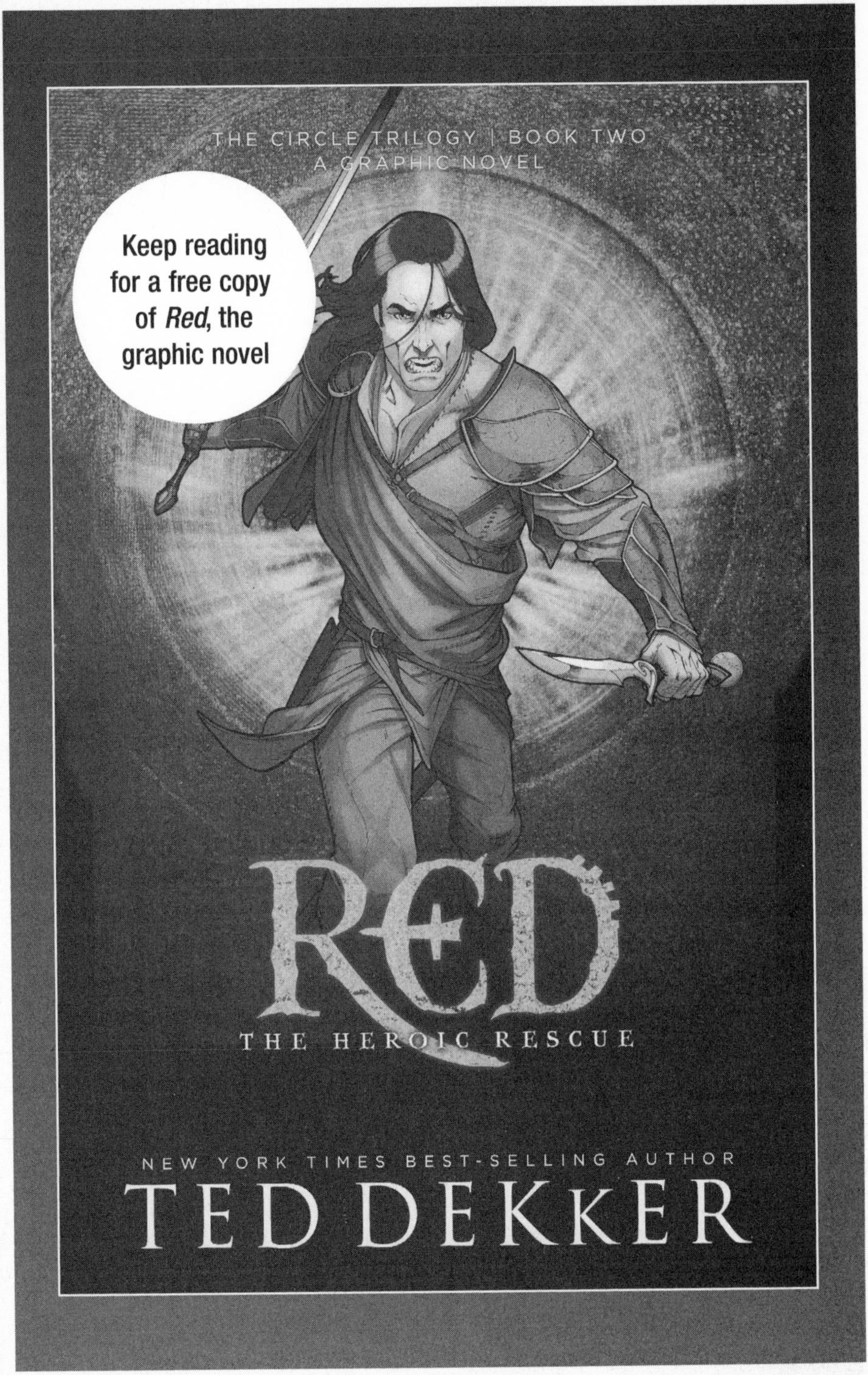

THE CIRCLE TRILOGY | BOOK TWO
A GRAPHIC NOVEL
Keep reading for a free copy of *Red*, the graphic novel
RED
THE HEROIC RESCUE
NEW YORK TIMES BEST-SELLING AUTHOR
TED DEKKER

Red Graphic Novel

Written by Ted Dekker

Adapted by Matt Hansen

Edited by Kevin Kaiser

Art by Ricardo Ratton, Eduardo Pansica, and Newton Barbosa

Colors by Giovanna Guimarães, Éber Ferreira, José Carlos,
and Gulliver Vianei

Lettered by Bill Tortolini

Front Cover Art by Mike S. Miller

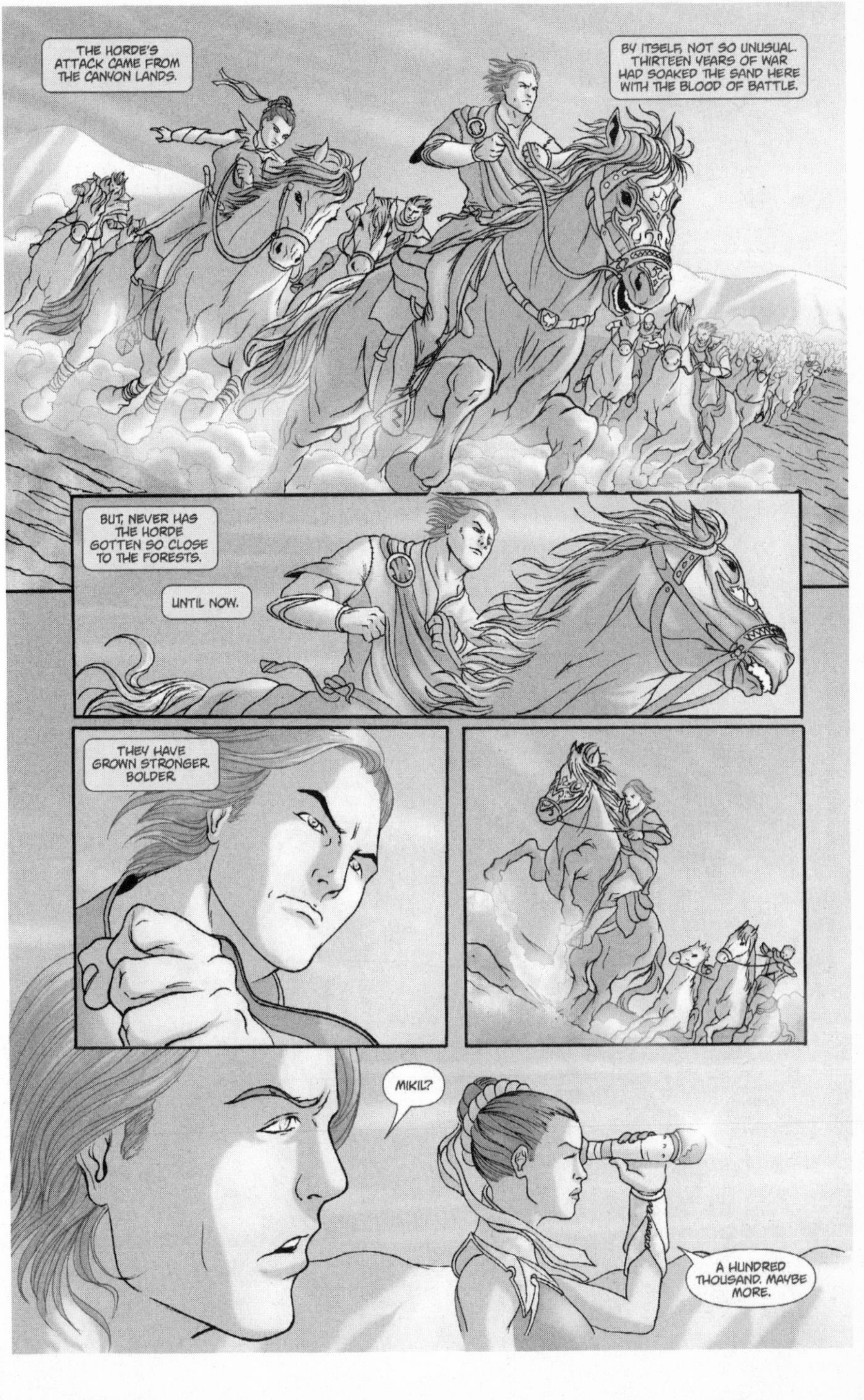
THE HORDE'S ATTACK CAME FROM THE CANYON LANDS.
BY ITSELF, NOT SO UNUSUAL. THIRTEEN YEARS OF WAR HAD SOAKED THE SAND HERE WITH THE BLOOD OF BATTLE.
BUT, NEVER HAS THE HORDE GOTTEN SO CLOSE TO THE FORESTS.
UNTIL NOW.
THEY HAVE GROWN STRONGER. BOLDER.
MIKIL?
A HUNDRED THOUSAND. MAYBE MORE.

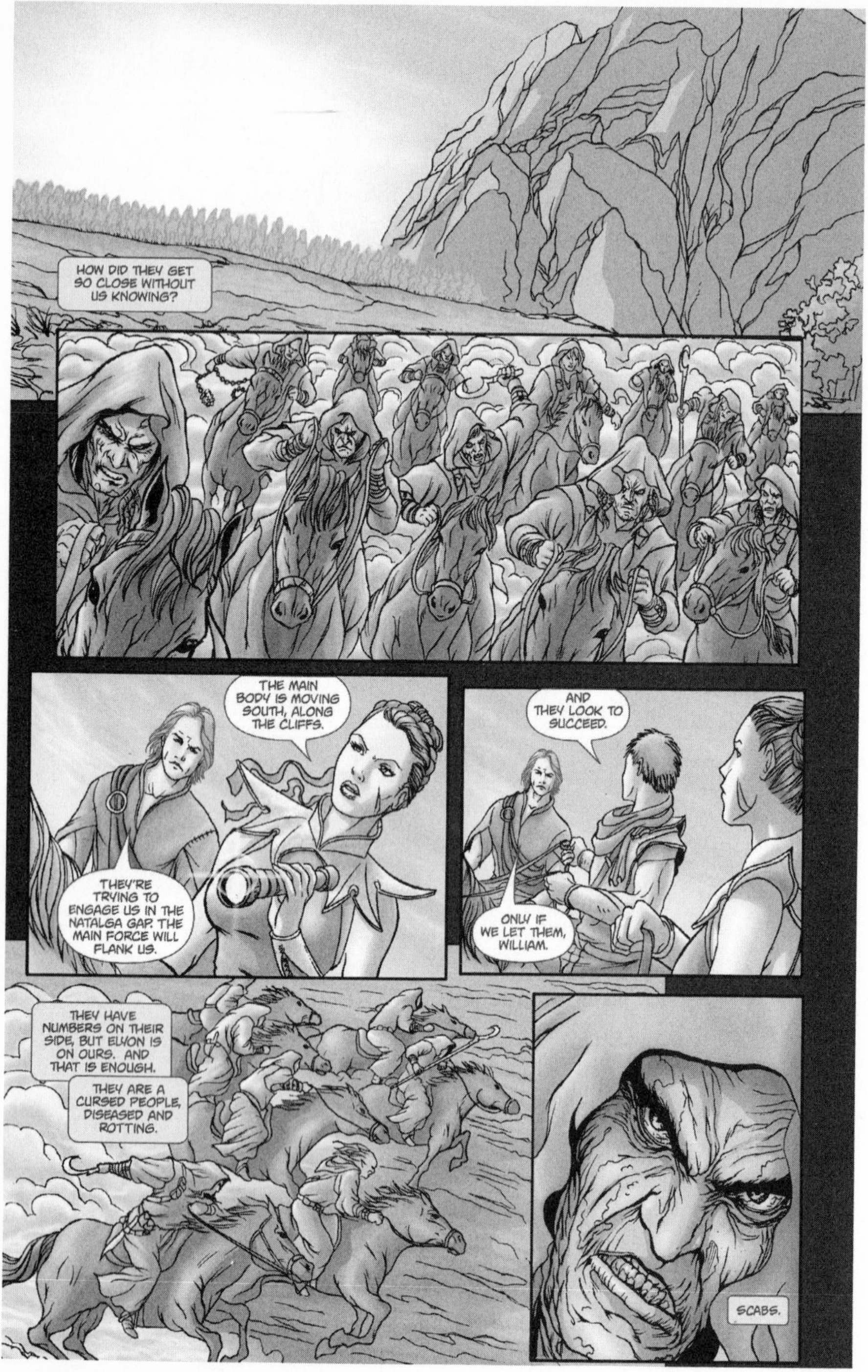
HOW DID THEY GET SO CLOSE WITHOUT US KNOWING?
THE MAIN BODY IS MOVING SOUTH, ALONG THE CLIFFS.
THEY'RE TRYING TO ENGAGE US IN THE NATALGA GAP. THE MAIN FORCE WILL FLANK US.
AND THEY LOOK TO SUCCEED.
ONLY IF WE LET THEM, WILLIAM.
THEY HAVE NUMBERS ON THEIR SIDE, BUT ELYON IS ON OURS. AND THAT IS ENOUGH.
THEY ARE A CURSED PEOPLE, DISEASED AND ROTTING.
SCABS.

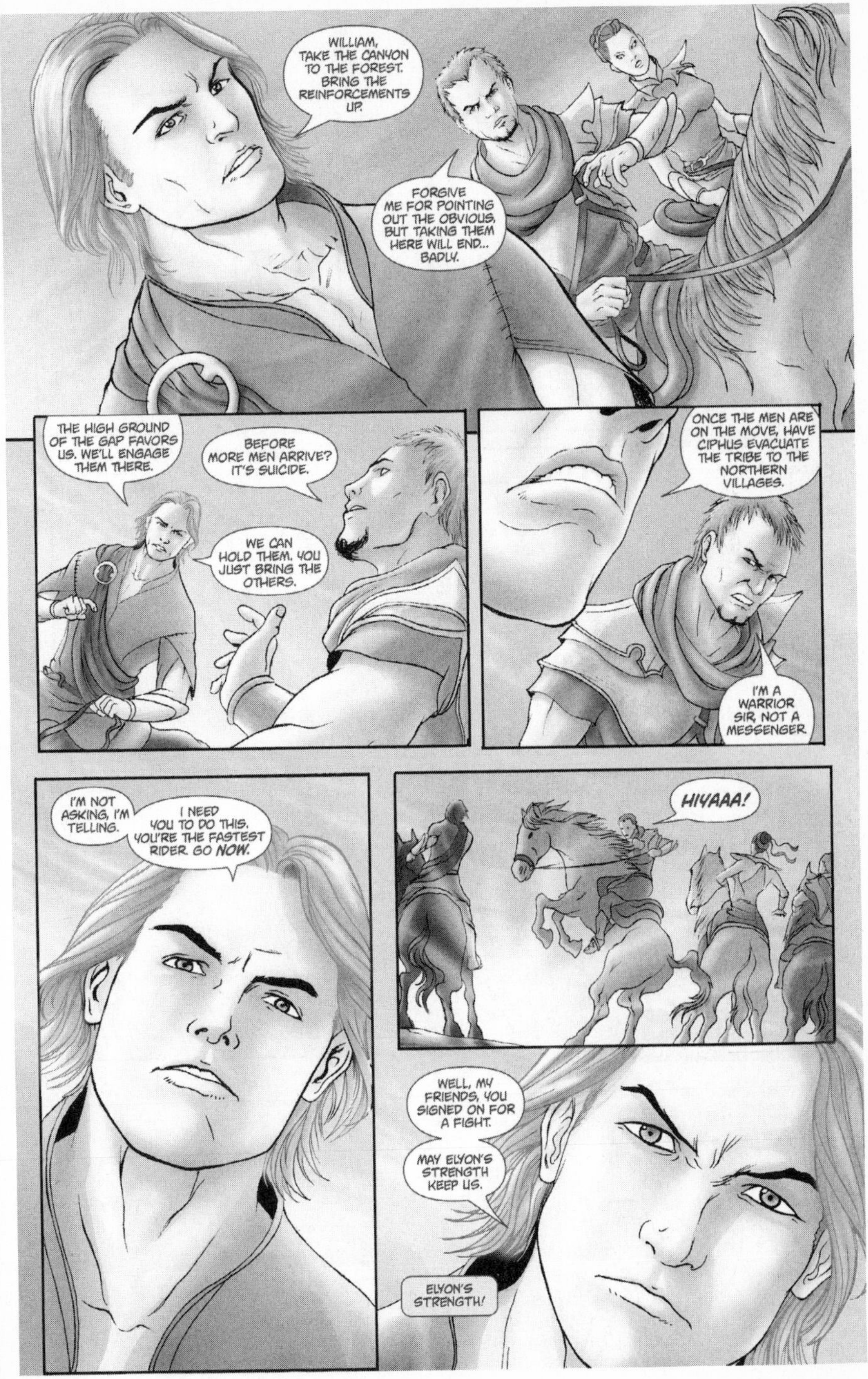
WILLIAM, TAKE THE CANYON TO THE FOREST. BRING THE REINFORCEMENTS UP.
FORGIVE ME FOR POINTING OUT THE OBVIOUS, BUT TAKING THEM HERE WILL END... BADLY.
THE HIGH GROUND OF THE GAP FAVORS US. WE'LL ENGAGE THEM THERE.
BEFORE MORE MEN ARRIVE? IT'S SUICIDE.
WE CAN HOLD THEM. YOU JUST BRING THE OTHERS.
ONCE THE MEN ARE ON THE MOVE, HAVE CIPHUS EVACUATE THE TRIBE TO THE NORTHERN VILLAGES.
I'M A WARRIOR SIR, NOT A MESSENGER.
I'M NOT ASKING, I'M TELLING.
I NEED YOU TO DO THIS. YOU'RE THE FASTEST RIDER. GO *NOW*.
HIYAAA!
WELL, MY FRIENDS, YOU SIGNED ON FOR A FIGHT.
MAY ELYON'S STRENGTH KEEP US.
ELYON'S STRENGTH!

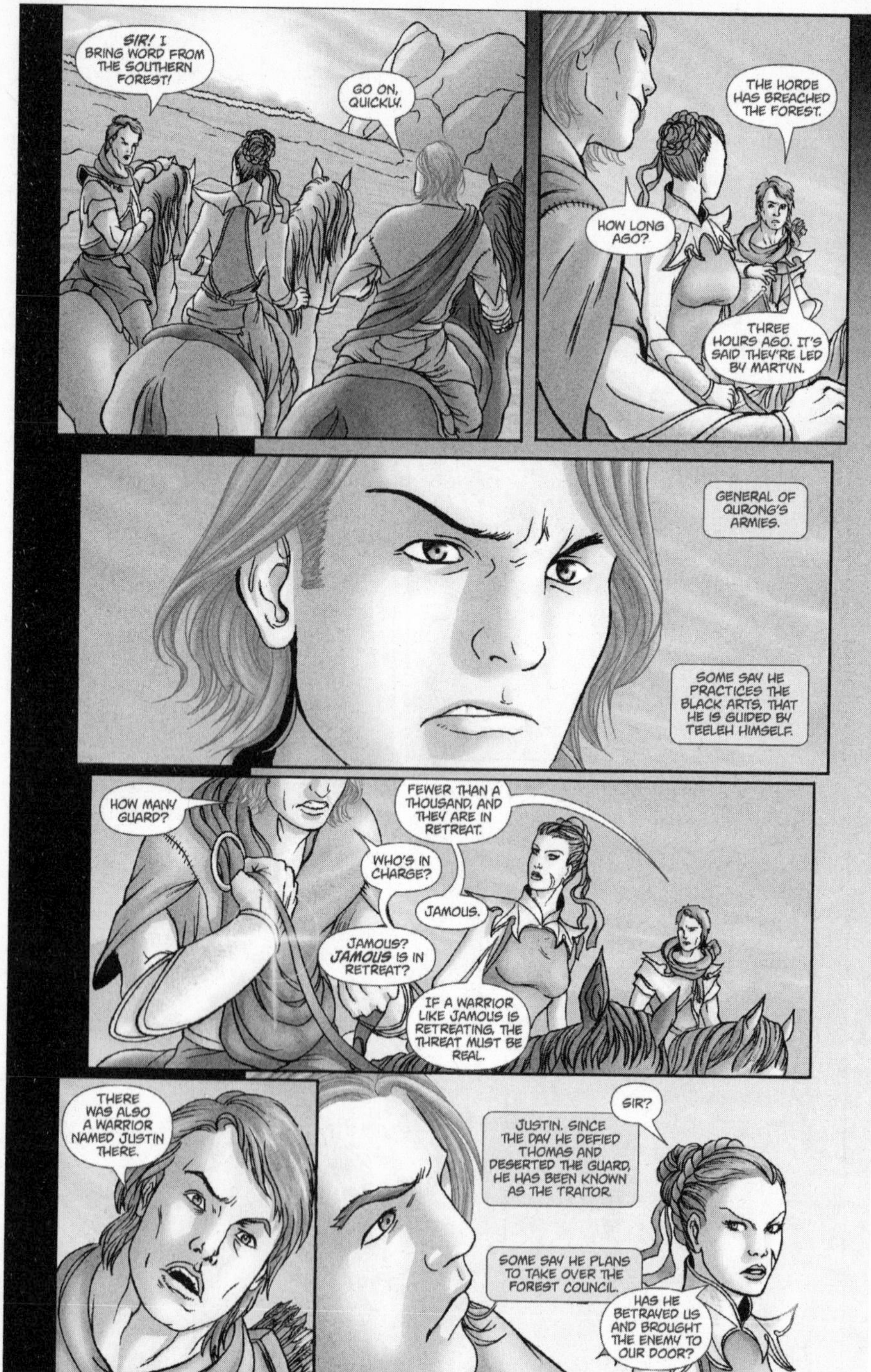
SIR! I BRING WORD FROM THE SOUTHERN FOREST!
GO ON, QUICKLY.
THE HORDE HAS BREACHED THE FOREST.
HOW LONG AGO?
THREE HOURS AGO. IT'S SAID THEY'RE LED BY MARTYN.
GENERAL OF QURONG'S ARMIES.
SOME SAY HE PRACTICES THE BLACK ARTS, THAT HE IS GUIDED BY TEELEH HIMSELF.
HOW MANY GUARD?
FEWER THAN A THOUSAND, AND THEY ARE IN RETREAT.
WHO'S IN CHARGE?
JAMOUS.
JAMOUS? JAMOUS IS IN RETREAT?
IF A WARRIOR LIKE JAMOUS IS RETREATING, THE THREAT MUST BE REAL.
THERE WAS ALSO A WARRIOR NAMED JUSTIN THERE.
JUSTIN. SINCE THE DAY HE DEFIED THOMAS AND DESERTED THE GUARD, HE HAS BEEN KNOWN AS THE TRAITOR.
SIR?
SOME SAY HE PLANS TO TAKE OVER THE FOREST COUNCIL.
HAS HE BETRAYED US AND BROUGHT THE ENEMY TO OUR DOOR?

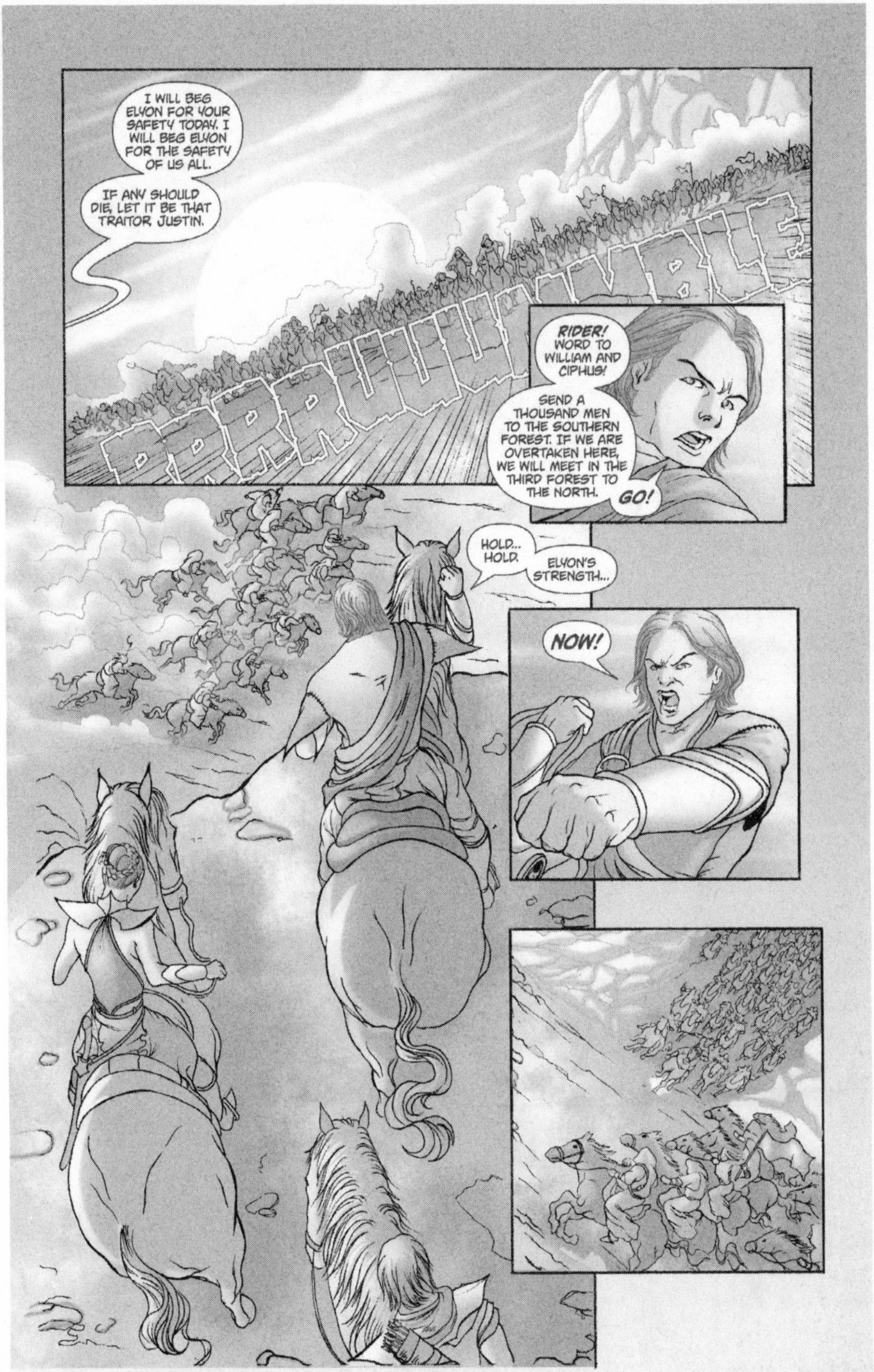

I WILL BEG ELYON FOR YOUR SAFETY TODAY. I WILL BEG ELYON FOR THE SAFETY OF US ALL.
IF ANY SHOULD DIE, LET IT BE THAT TRAITOR, JUSTIN.
BRRRUUUMMBLE
RIDER! WORD TO WILLIAM AND CIPHUS!
SEND A THOUSAND MEN TO THE SOUTHERN FOREST. IF WE ARE OVERTAKEN HERE, WE WILL MEET IN THE THIRD FOREST TO THE NORTH. GO!
HOLD... HOLD.
ELYON'S STRENGTH...
NOW!

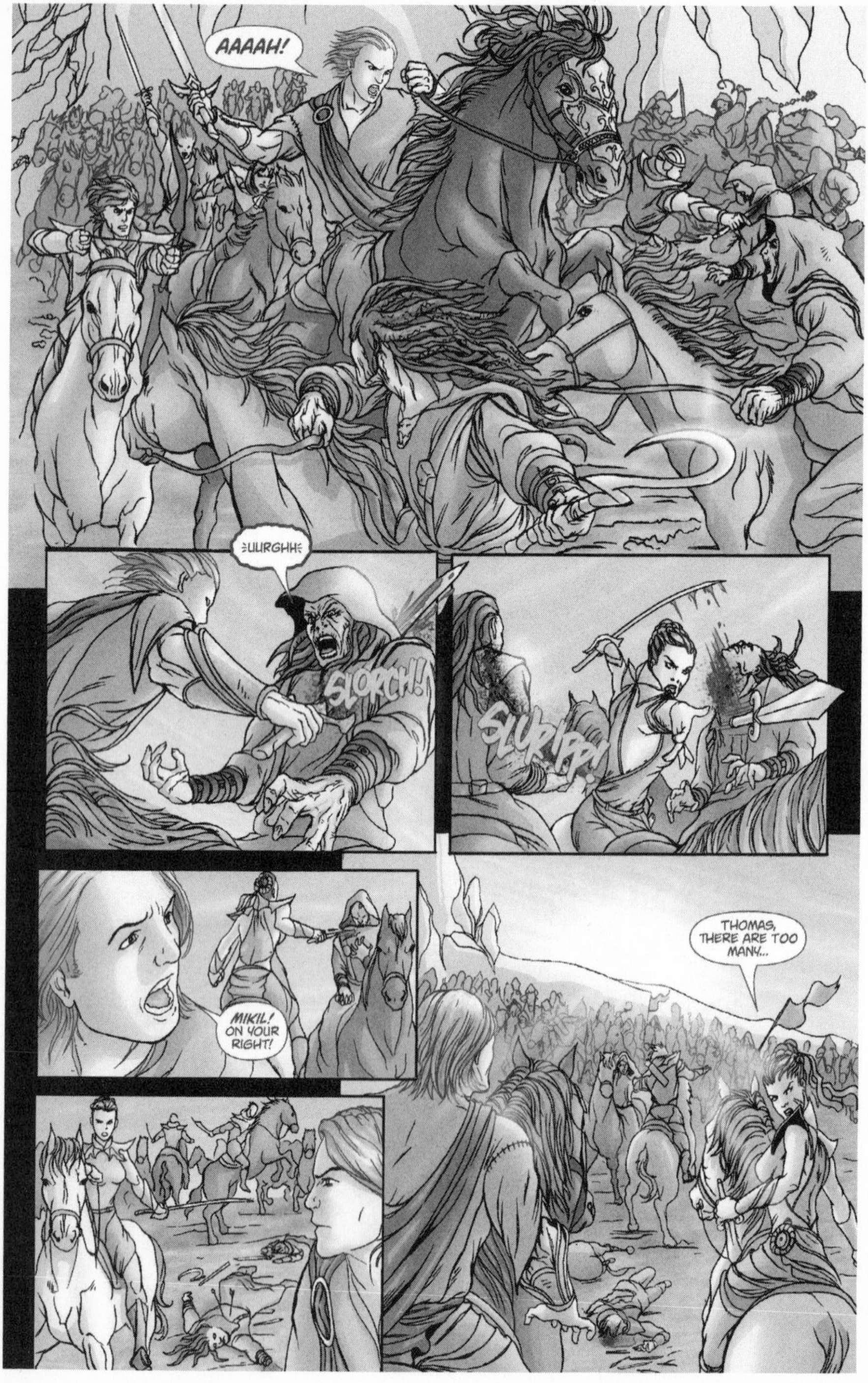
AAAAH!
UURGHH
SLORCH!
SLURPP!
MIKIL! ON YOUR RIGHT!
THOMAS, THERE ARE TOO MANY...

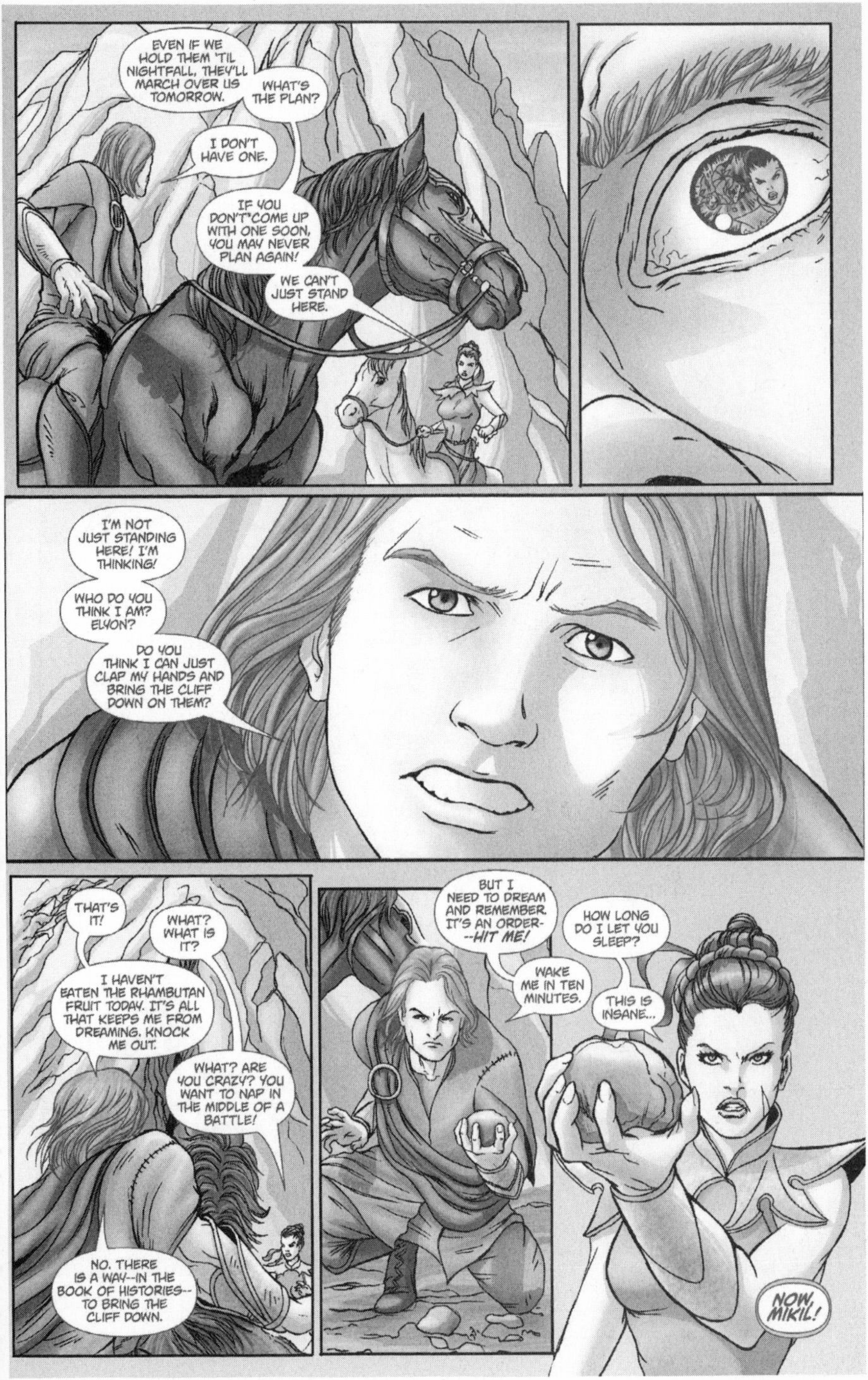
EVEN IF WE HOLD THEM 'TIL NIGHTFALL, THEY'LL MARCH OVER US TOMORROW.
WHAT'S THE PLAN?
I DON'T HAVE ONE.
IF YOU DON'T COME UP WITH ONE SOON, YOU MAY NEVER PLAN AGAIN!
WE CAN'T JUST STAND HERE.
I'M NOT JUST STANDING HERE! I'M THINKING!
WHO DO YOU THINK I AM? ELYON?
DO YOU THINK I CAN JUST CLAP MY HANDS AND BRING THE CLIFF DOWN ON THEM?
THAT'S IT!
WHAT? WHAT IS IT?
I HAVEN'T EATEN THE RHAMBUTAN FRUIT TODAY. IT'S ALL THAT KEEPS ME FROM DREAMING. KNOCK ME OUT.
WHAT? ARE YOU CRAZY? YOU WANT TO NAP IN THE MIDDLE OF A BATTLE!
NO. THERE IS A WAY--IN THE BOOK OF HISTORIES--TO BRING THE CLIFF DOWN.
BUT I NEED TO DREAM AND REMEMBER. IT'S AN ORDER--HIT ME!
WAKE ME IN TEN MINUTES.
HOW LONG DO I LET YOU SLEEP?
THIS IS INSANE...
NOW, MIKIL!

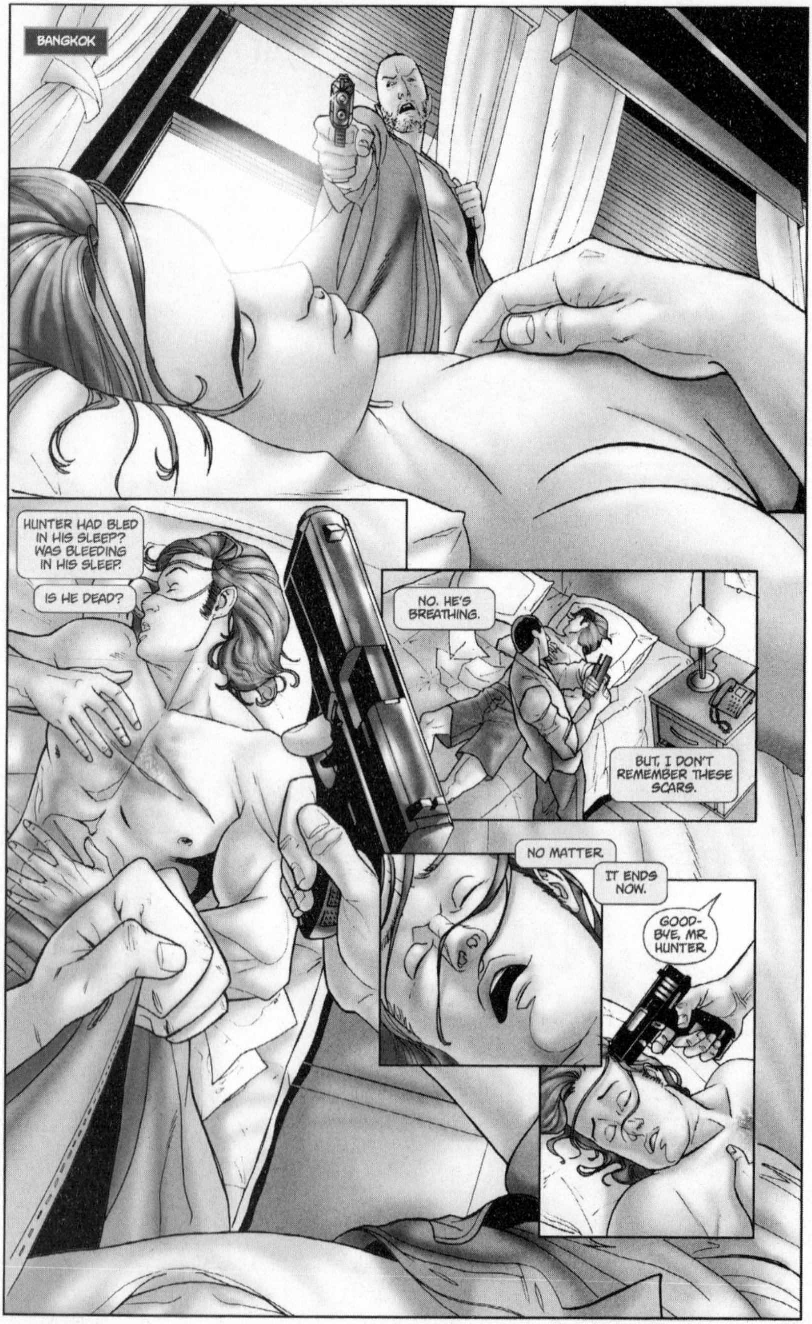
BANGKOK
HUNTER HAD BLED IN HIS SLEEP? WAS BLEEDING IN HIS SLEEP.
IS HE DEAD?
NO. HE'S BREATHING.
BUT, I DON'T REMEMBER THESE SCARS.
NO MATTER.
IT ENDS NOW.
GOOD-BYE, MR. HUNTER.

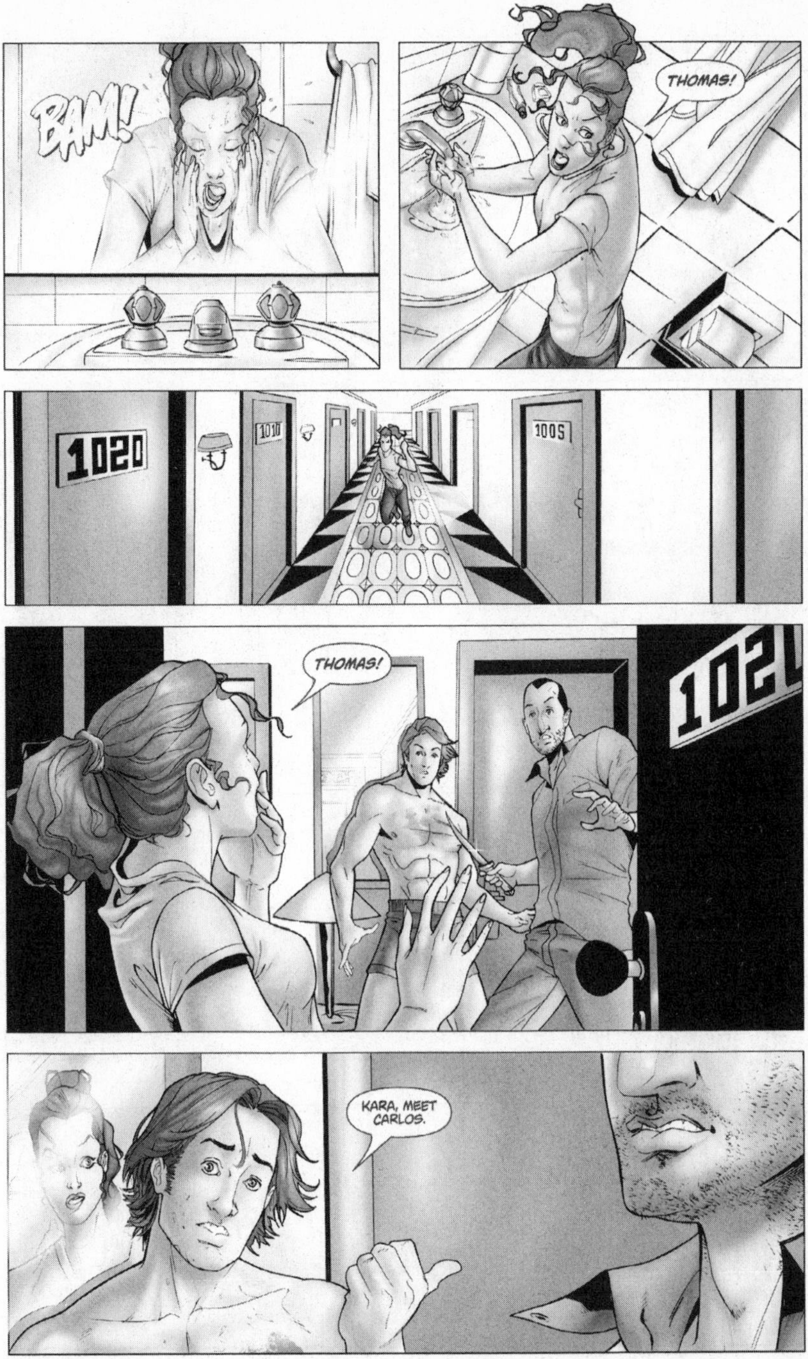
BAM!
THOMAS!
1020
1010
1005
THOMAS!
KARA, MEET CARLOS.

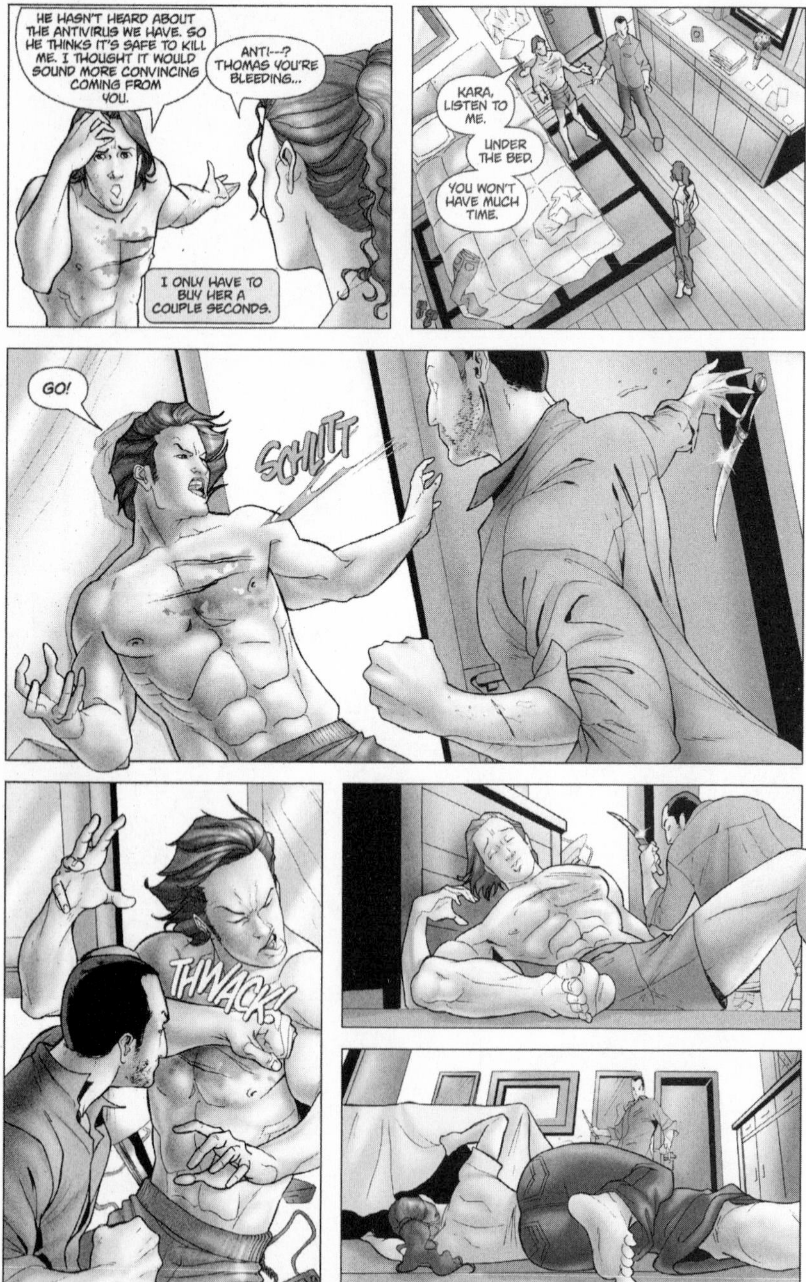
HE HASN'T HEARD ABOUT THE ANTIVIRUS WE HAVE. SO HE THINKS IT'S SAFE TO KILL ME. I THOUGHT IT WOULD SOUND MORE CONVINCING COMING FROM YOU.
ANTI--? THOMAS YOU'RE BLEEDING...
I ONLY HAVE TO BUY HER A COUPLE SECONDS.
KARA, LISTEN TO ME.
UNDER THE BED.
YOU WON'T HAVE MUCH TIME.
GO!
SCHLITT
THWACK!

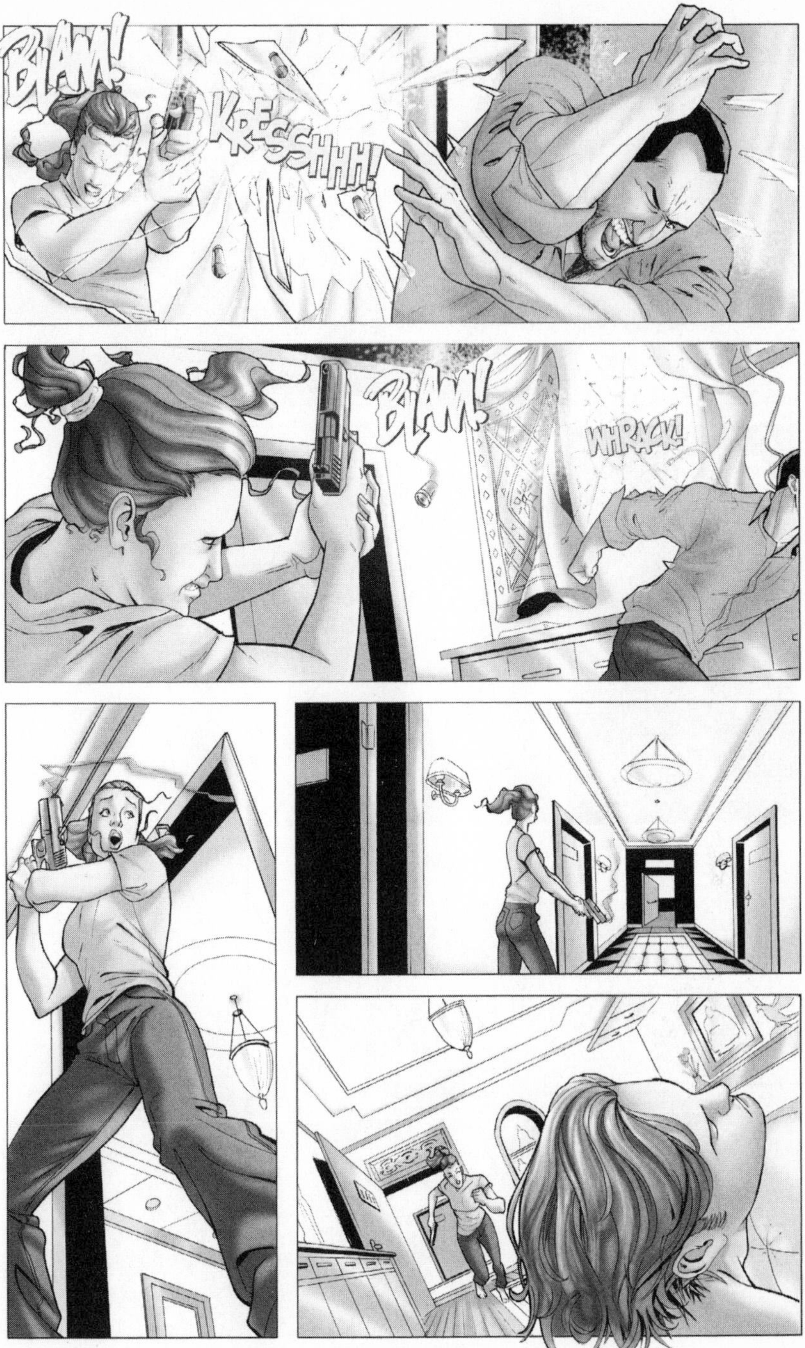
BLAM!
KRESSHHH!
BLAM!
WHRACK!

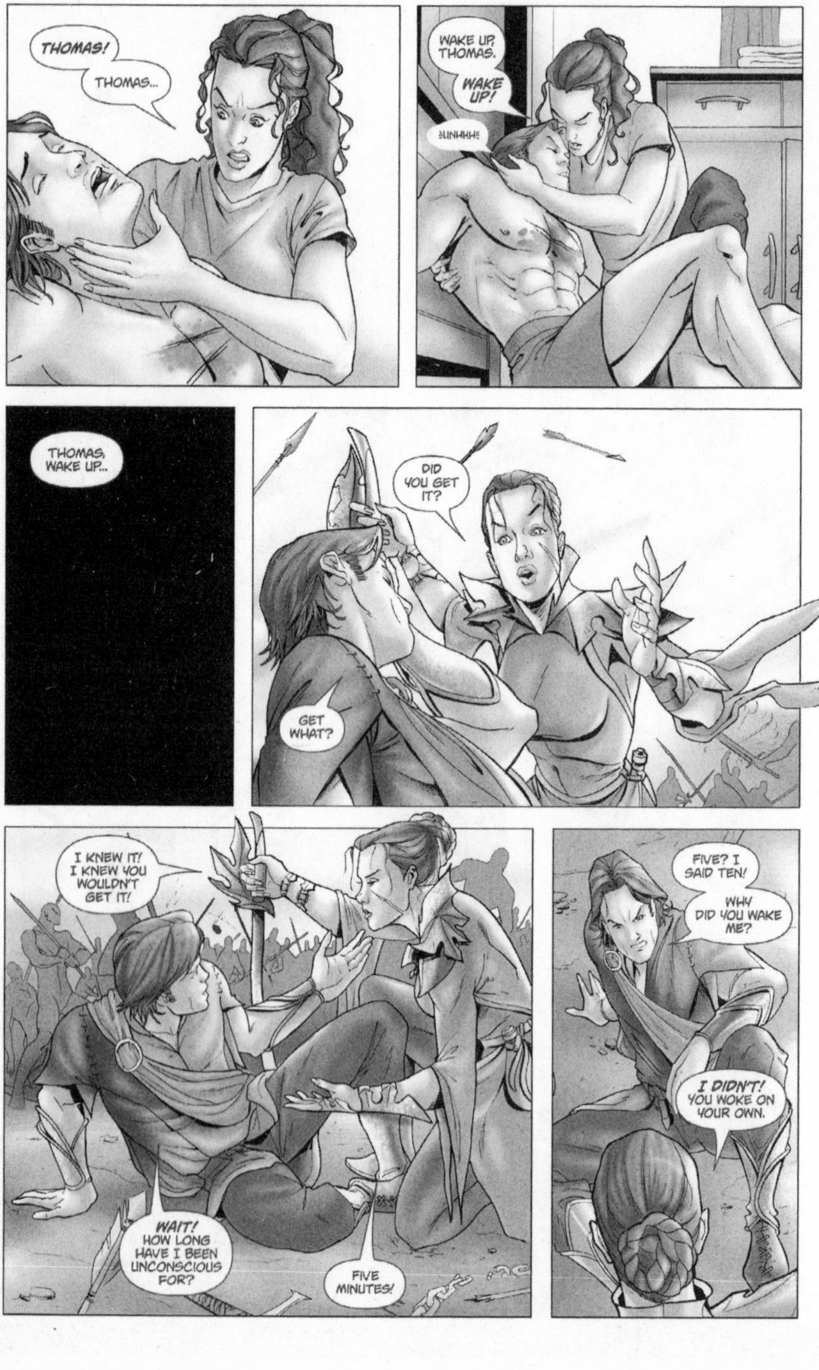
THOMAS!
THOMAS...
WAKE UP, THOMAS.
WAKE UP!
UNHHH
THOMAS, WAKE UP...
DID YOU GET IT?
GET WHAT?
I KNEW IT! I KNEW YOU WOULDN'T GET IT!
WAIT! HOW LONG HAVE I BEEN UNCONSCIOUS FOR?
FIVE MINUTES!
FIVE? I SAID TEN!
WHY DID YOU WAKE ME?
I DIDN'T! YOU WOKE ON YOUR OWN.

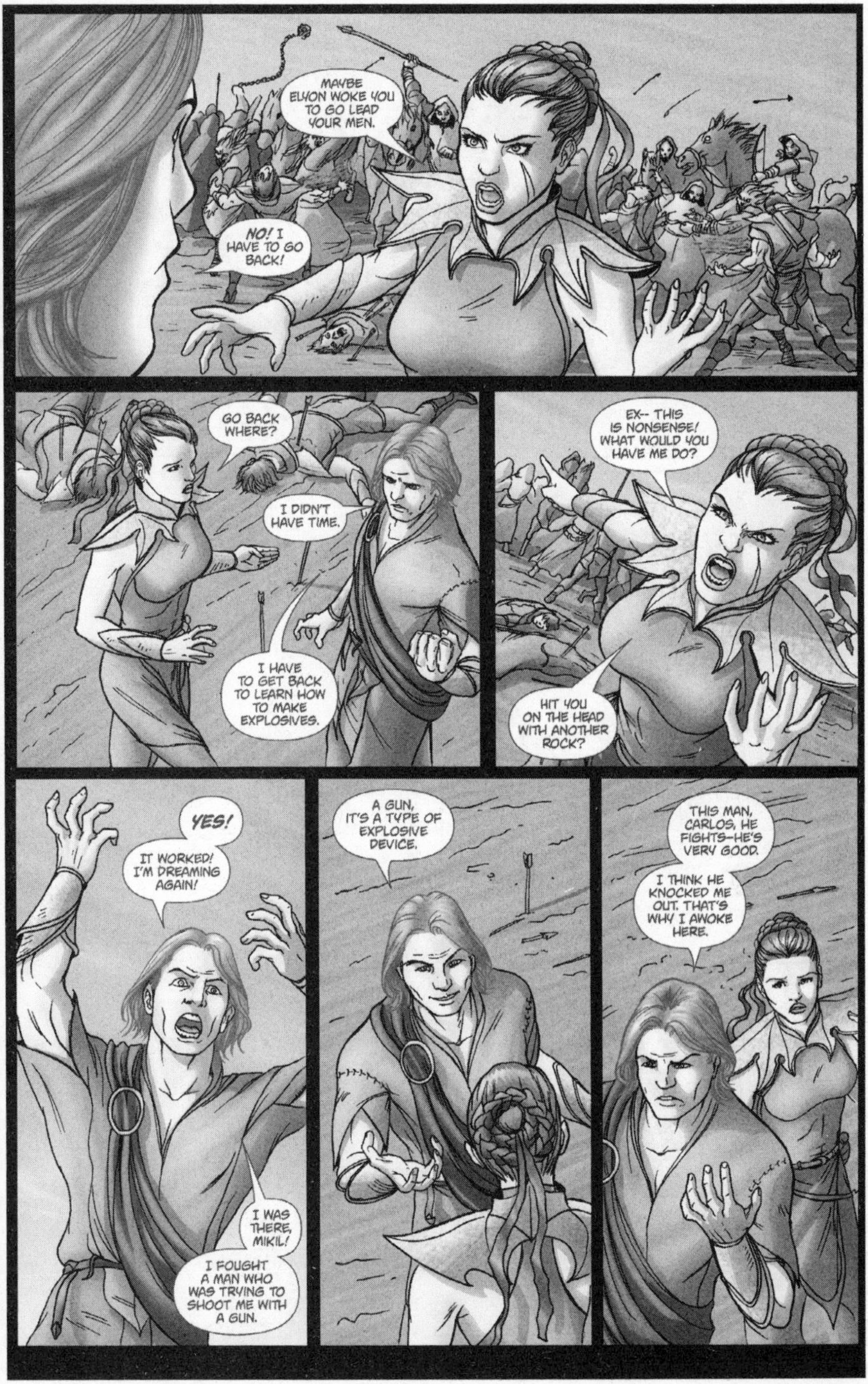
MAYBE ELYON WOKE YOU TO GO LEAD YOUR MEN.
NO! I HAVE TO GO BACK!
GO BACK WHERE?
I DIDN'T HAVE TIME.
I HAVE TO GET BACK TO LEARN HOW TO MAKE EXPLOSIVES.
EX-- THIS IS NONSENSE! WHAT WOULD YOU HAVE ME DO?
HIT YOU ON THE HEAD WITH ANOTHER ROCK?
YES!
IT WORKED! I'M DREAMING AGAIN!
I WAS THERE, MIKIL!
I FOUGHT A MAN WHO WAS TRYING TO SHOOT ME WITH A GUN.
A GUN, IT'S A TYPE OF EXPLOSIVE DEVICE.
THIS MAN, CARLOS, HE FIGHTS—HE'S VERY GOOD.
I THINK HE KNOCKED ME OUT. THAT'S WHY I AWOKE HERE.

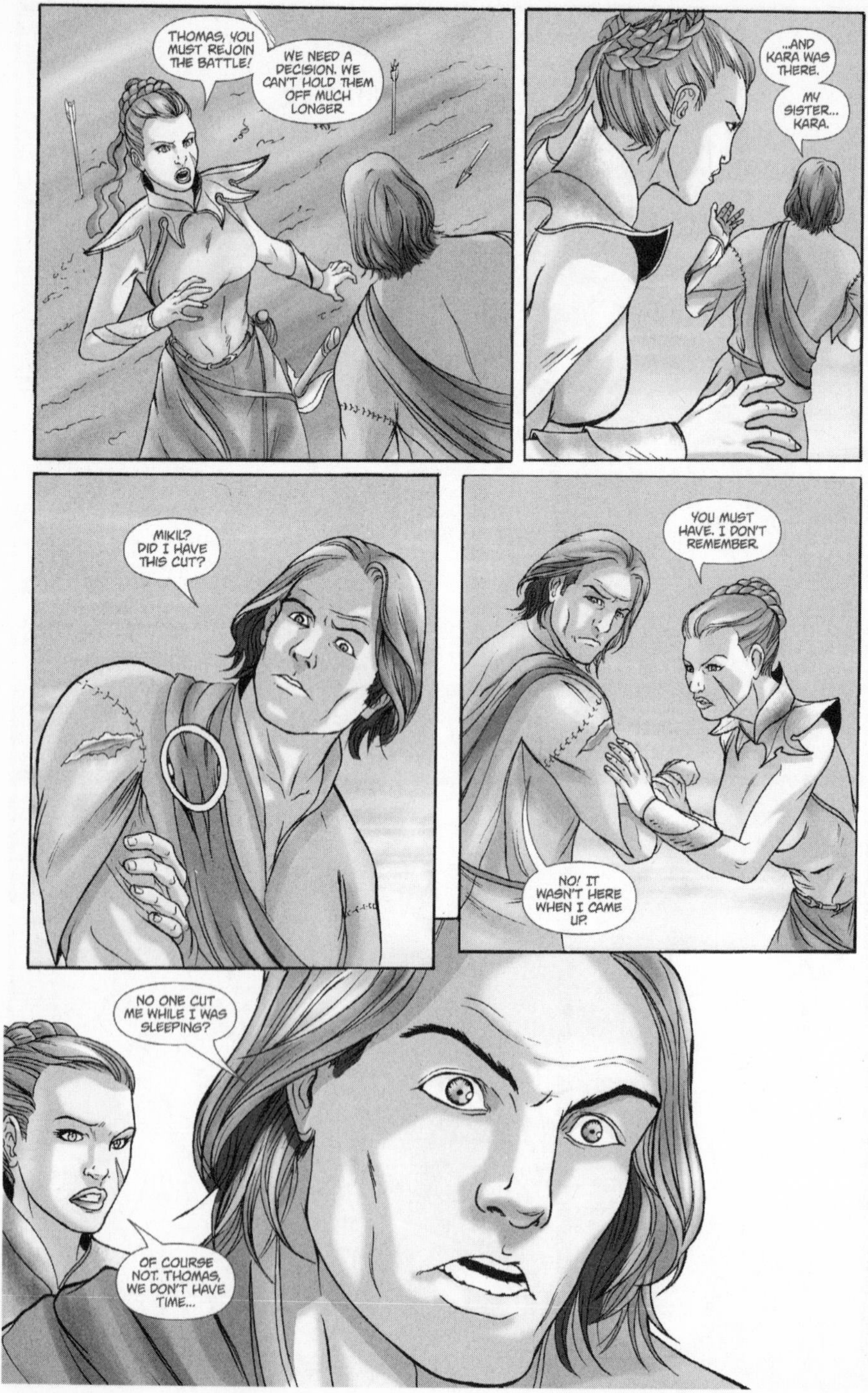
THOMAS, YOU MUST REJOIN THE BATTLE!
WE NEED A DECISION. WE CAN'T HOLD THEM OFF MUCH LONGER.
...AND KARA WAS THERE.
MY SISTER... KARA.
MIKIL? DID I HAVE THIS CUT?
YOU MUST HAVE. I DON'T REMEMBER.
NO! IT WASN'T HERE WHEN I CAME UP.
NO ONE CUT ME WHILE I WAS SLEEPING?
OF COURSE NOT. THOMAS, WE DON'T HAVE TIME...

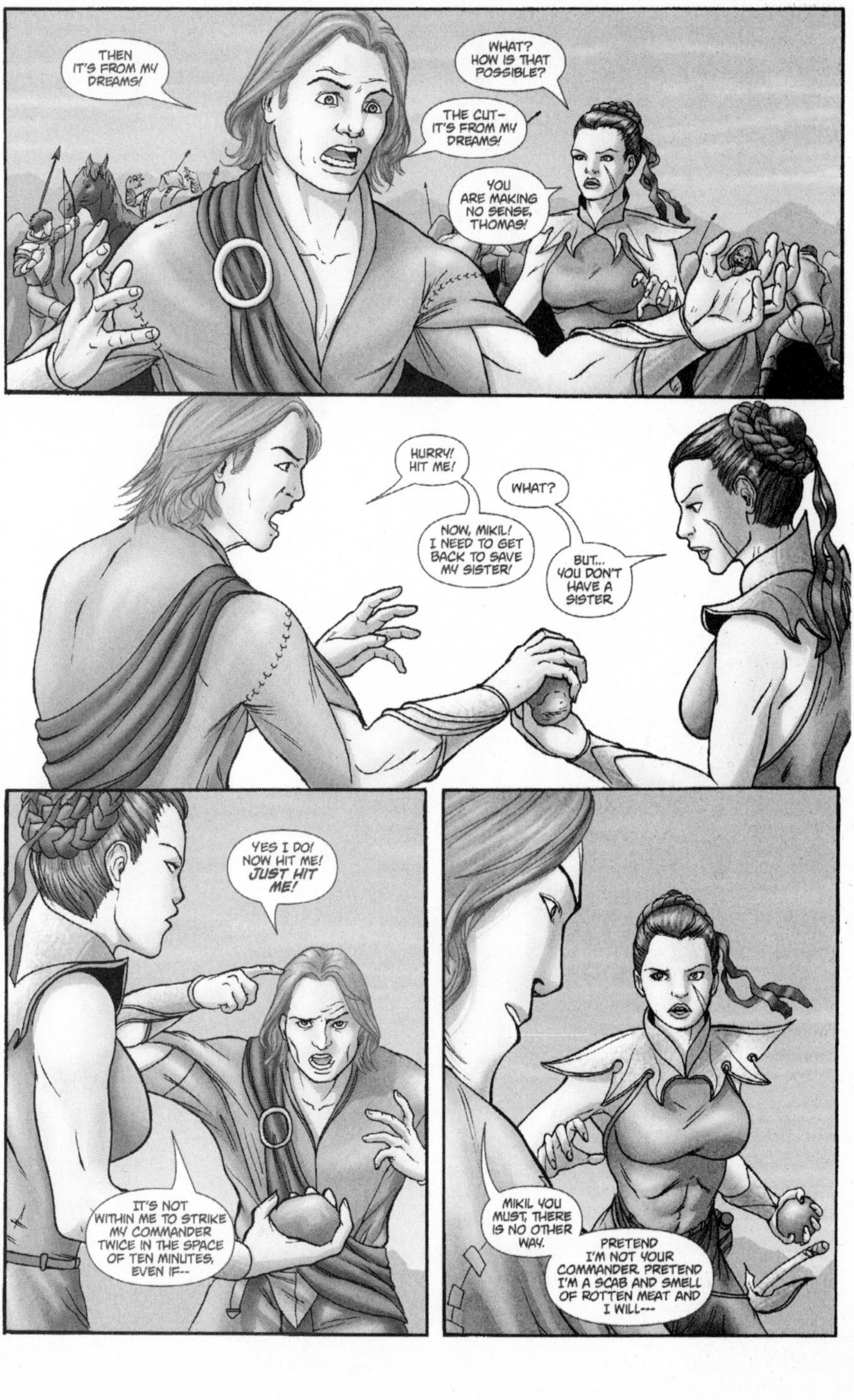
THEN IT'S FROM MY DREAMS!
WHAT? HOW IS THAT POSSIBLE?
THE CUT-- IT'S FROM MY DREAMS!
YOU ARE MAKING NO SENSE, THOMAS!
HURRY! HIT ME!
NOW, MIKIL! I NEED TO GET BACK TO SAVE MY SISTER!
WHAT?
BUT... YOU DON'T HAVE A SISTER
YES I DO! NOW HIT ME! JUST HIT ME!
IT'S NOT WITHIN ME TO STRIKE MY COMMANDER TWICE IN THE SPACE OF TEN MINUTES, EVEN IF--
MIKIL YOU MUST, THERE IS NO OTHER WAY.
PRETEND I'M NOT YOUR COMMANDER. PRETEND I'M A SCAB AND SMELL OF ROTTEN MEAT AND I WILL---

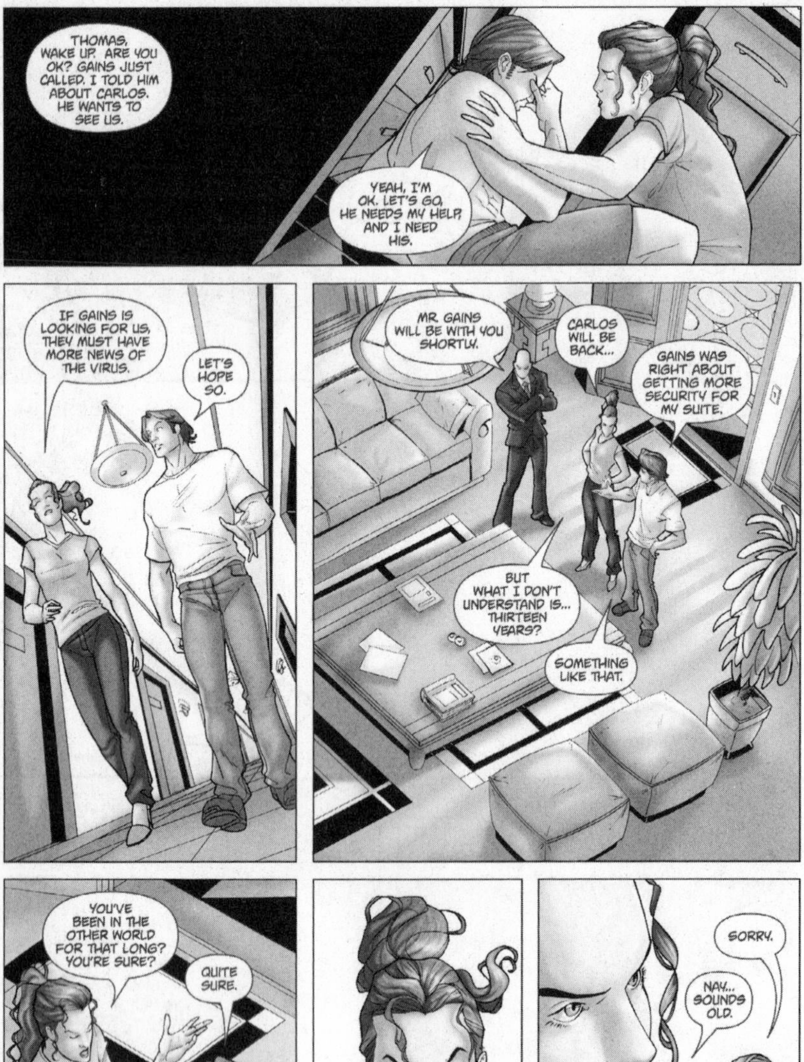
THOMAS, WAKE UP. ARE YOU OK? GAINS JUST CALLED. I TOLD HIM ABOUT CARLOS. HE WANTS TO SEE US.
YEAH, I'M OK. LET'S GO, HE NEEDS MY HELP, AND I NEED HIS.
IF GAINS IS LOOKING FOR US, THEY MUST HAVE MORE NEWS OF THE VIRUS.
LET'S HOPE SO.
MR. GAINS WILL BE WITH YOU SHORTLY.
CARLOS WILL BE BACK...
GAINS WAS RIGHT ABOUT GETTING MORE SECURITY FOR MY SUITE.
BUT WHAT I DON'T UNDERSTAND IS... THIRTEEN YEARS?
SOMETHING LIKE THAT.
YOU'VE BEEN IN THE OTHER WORLD FOR THAT LONG? YOU'RE SURE?
QUITE SURE.
HOW IS THAT POSSIBLE? YOU'RE NOT THIRTEEN YEARS OLDER, ARE YOU?
MY BODY ISN'T, NAY-
NAY?
SORRY.
NAY... SOUNDS OLD.

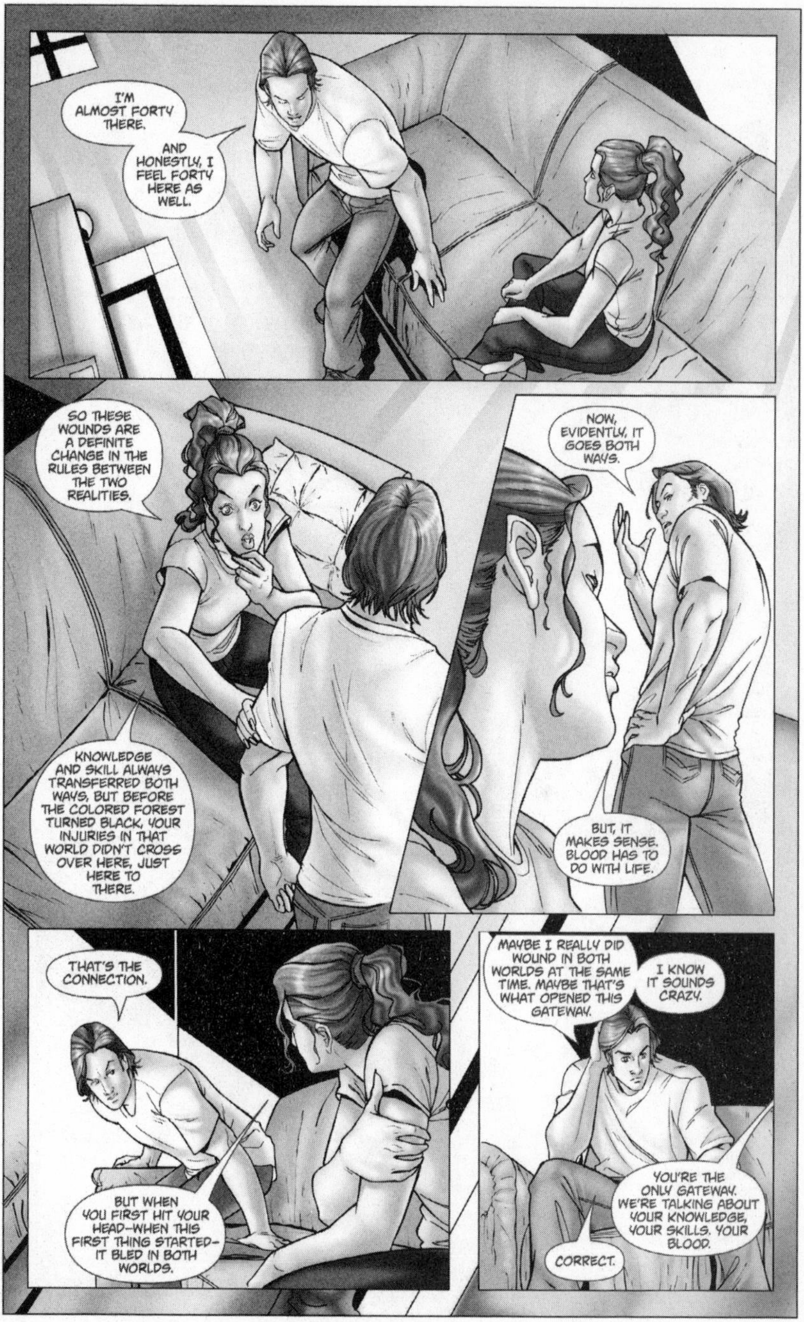
I'M ALMOST FORTY THERE.
AND HONESTLY, I FEEL FORTY HERE AS WELL.
SO THESE WOUNDS ARE A DEFINITE CHANGE IN THE RULES BETWEEN THE TWO REALITIES.
KNOWLEDGE AND SKILL ALWAYS TRANSFERRED BOTH WAYS, BUT BEFORE THE COLORED FOREST TURNED BLACK, YOUR INJURIES IN THAT WORLD DIDN'T CROSS OVER HERE, JUST HERE TO THERE.
NOW, EVIDENTLY, IT GOES BOTH WAYS.
BUT, IT MAKES SENSE. BLOOD HAS TO DO WITH LIFE.
THAT'S THE CONNECTION.
BUT WHEN YOU FIRST HIT YOUR HEAD–WHEN THIS FIRST THING STARTED–IT BLED IN BOTH WORLDS.
MAYBE I REALLY DID WOUND IN BOTH WORLDS AT THE SAME TIME. MAYBE THAT'S WHAT OPENED THIS GATEWAY.
I KNOW IT SOUNDS CRAZY.
YOU'RE THE ONLY GATEWAY. WE'RE TALKING ABOUT YOUR KNOWLEDGE, YOUR SKILLS. YOUR BLOOD.
CORRECT.

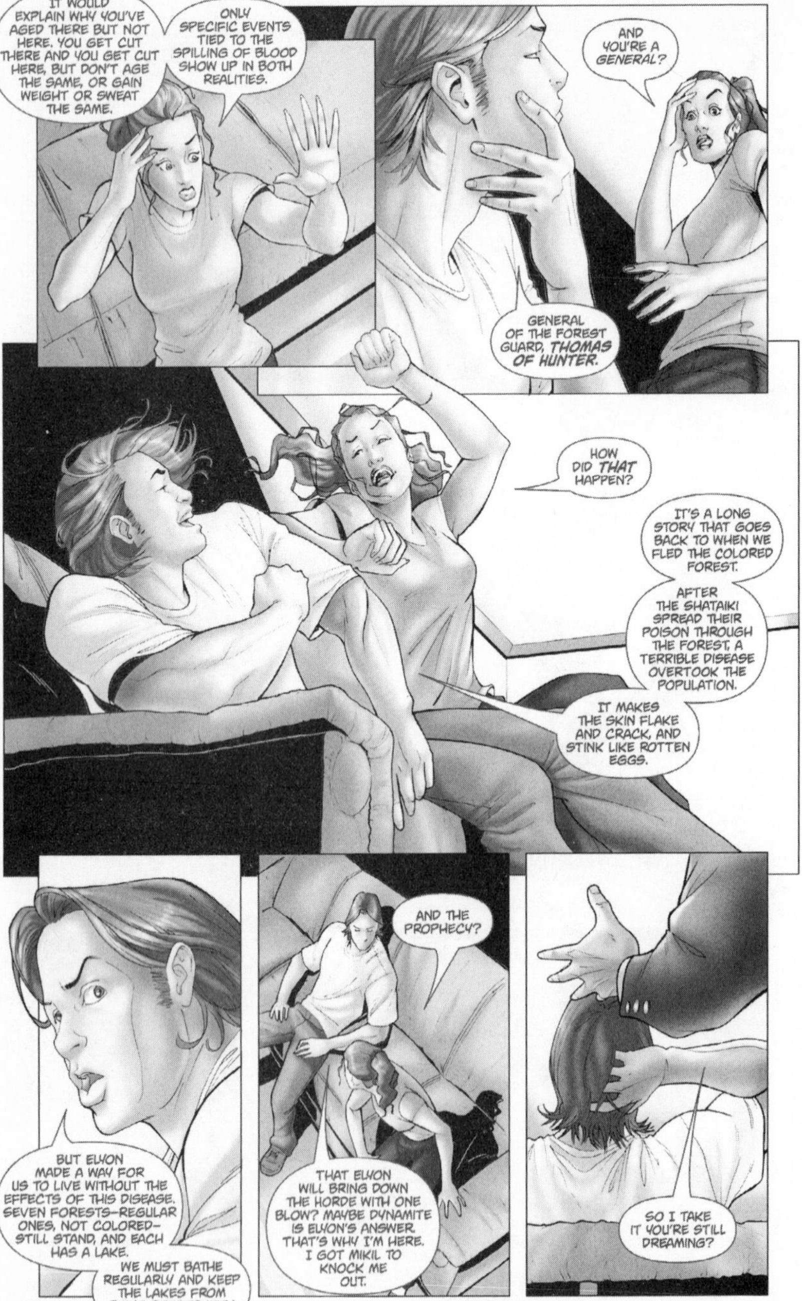

IT WOULD EXPLAIN WHY YOU'VE AGED THERE BUT NOT HERE. YOU GET CUT THERE AND YOU GET CUT HERE, BUT DON'T AGE THE SAME, OR GAIN WEIGHT OR SWEAT THE SAME.
ONLY SPECIFIC EVENTS TIED TO THE SPILLING OF BLOOD SHOW UP IN BOTH REALITIES.
AND YOU'RE A GENERAL?
GENERAL OF THE FOREST GUARD, THOMAS OF HUNTER.
HOW DID THAT HAPPEN?
IT'S A LONG STORY THAT GOES BACK TO WHEN WE FLED THE COLORED FOREST.
AFTER THE SHATAIKI SPREAD THEIR POISON THROUGH THE FOREST, A TERRIBLE DISEASE OVERTOOK THE POPULATION.
IT MAKES THE SKIN FLAKE AND CRACK, AND STINK LIKE ROTTEN EGGS.
BUT ELYON MADE A WAY FOR US TO LIVE WITHOUT THE EFFECTS OF THIS DISEASE. SEVEN FORESTS—REGULAR ONES, NOT COLORED—STILL STAND, AND EACH HAS A LAKE.
WE MUST BATHE REGULARLY AND KEEP THE LAKES FROM BEING DEFILED WITH BLOOD.
AND THE PROPHECY?
THAT ELYON WILL BRING DOWN THE HORDE WITH ONE BLOW? MAYBE DYNAMITE IS ELYON'S ANSWER. THAT'S WHY I'M HERE. I GOT MIKIL TO KNOCK ME OUT.
SO I TAKE IT YOU'RE STILL DREAMING?

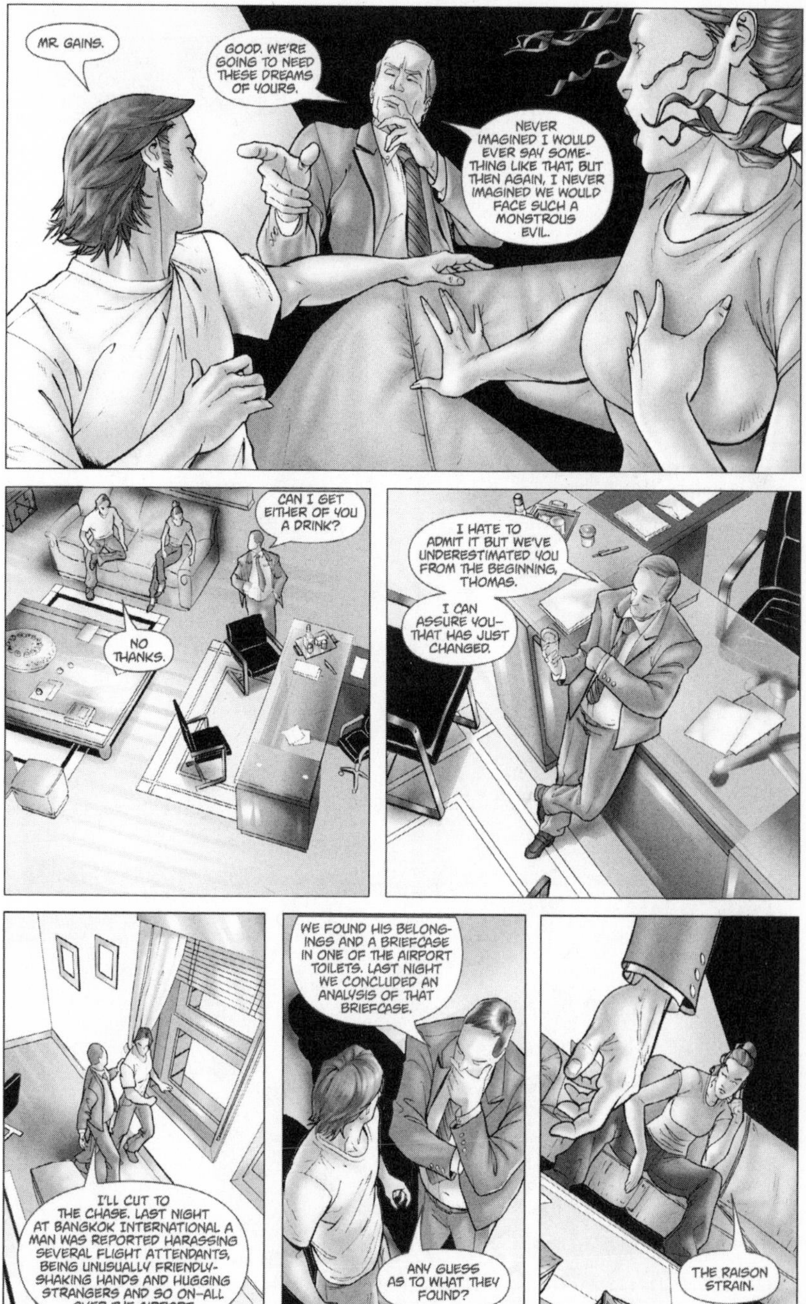
MR. GAINS.
GOOD. WE'RE GOING TO NEED THESE DREAMS OF YOURS.
NEVER IMAGINED I WOULD EVER SAY SOME-THING LIKE THAT, BUT THEN AGAIN, I NEVER IMAGINED WE WOULD FACE SUCH A MONSTROUS EVIL.
CAN I GET EITHER OF YOU A DRINK?
NO THANKS.
I HATE TO ADMIT IT BUT WE'VE UNDERESTIMATED YOU FROM THE BEGINNING, THOMAS.
I CAN ASSURE YOU— THAT HAS JUST CHANGED.
I'LL CUT TO THE CHASE. LAST NIGHT AT BANGKOK INTERNATIONAL A MAN WAS REPORTED HARASSING SEVERAL FLIGHT ATTENDANTS, BEING UNUSUALLY FRIENDLY-SHAKING HANDS AND HUGGING STRANGERS AND SO ON—ALL OVER THE AIRPORT.
WE FOUND HIS BELONG-INGS AND A BRIEFCASE IN ONE OF THE AIRPORT TOILETS. LAST NIGHT WE CONCLUDED AN ANALYSIS OF THAT BRIEFCASE.
ANY GUESS AS TO WHAT THEY FOUND?
THE RAISON STRAIN.

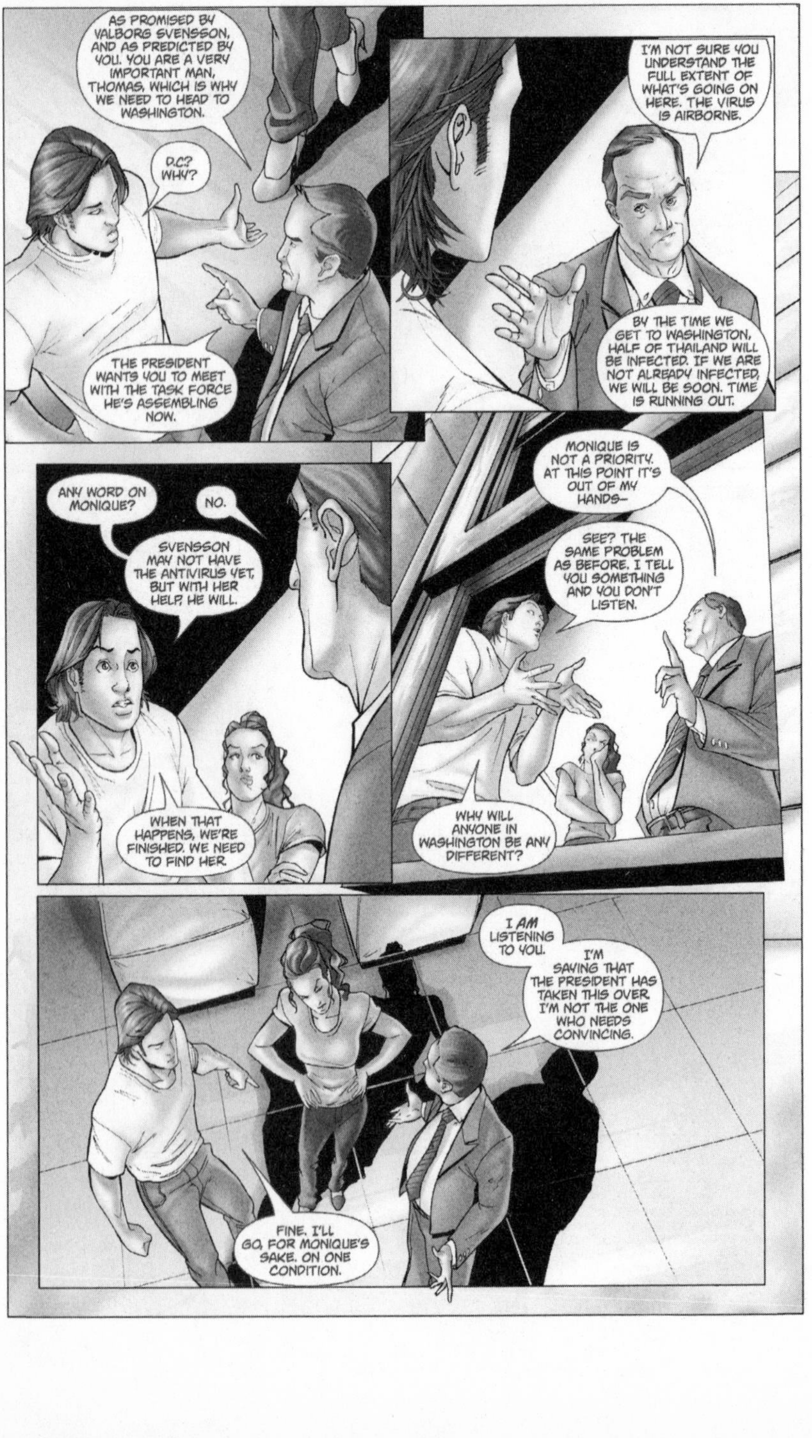
AS PROMISED BY VALBORG SVENSSON, AND AS PREDICTED BY YOU. YOU ARE A VERY IMPORTANT MAN, THOMAS, WHICH IS WHY WE NEED TO HEAD TO WASHINGTON.
D.C? WHY?
THE PRESIDENT WANTS YOU TO MEET WITH THE TASK FORCE HE'S ASSEMBLING NOW.
I'M NOT SURE YOU UNDERSTAND THE FULL EXTENT OF WHAT'S GOING ON HERE. THE VIRUS IS AIRBORNE.
BY THE TIME WE GET TO WASHINGTON, HALF OF THAILAND WILL BE INFECTED. IF WE ARE NOT ALREADY INFECTED, WE WILL BE SOON. TIME IS RUNNING OUT.
ANY WORD ON MONIQUE?
NO.
SVENSSON MAY NOT HAVE THE ANTIVIRUS YET, BUT WITH HER HELP, HE WILL.
WHEN THAT HAPPENS, WE'RE FINISHED. WE NEED TO FIND HER.
MONIQUE IS NOT A PRIORITY. AT THIS POINT IT'S OUT OF MY HANDS–
SEE? THE SAME PROBLEM AS BEFORE. I TELL YOU SOMETHING AND YOU DON'T LISTEN.
WHY WILL ANYONE IN WASHINGTON BE ANY DIFFERENT?
I AM LISTENING TO YOU.
I'M SAYING THAT THE PRESIDENT HAS TAKEN THIS OVER. I'M NOT THE ONE WHO NEEDS CONVINCING.
FINE. I'LL GO, FOR MONIQUE'S SAKE. ON ONE CONDITION.

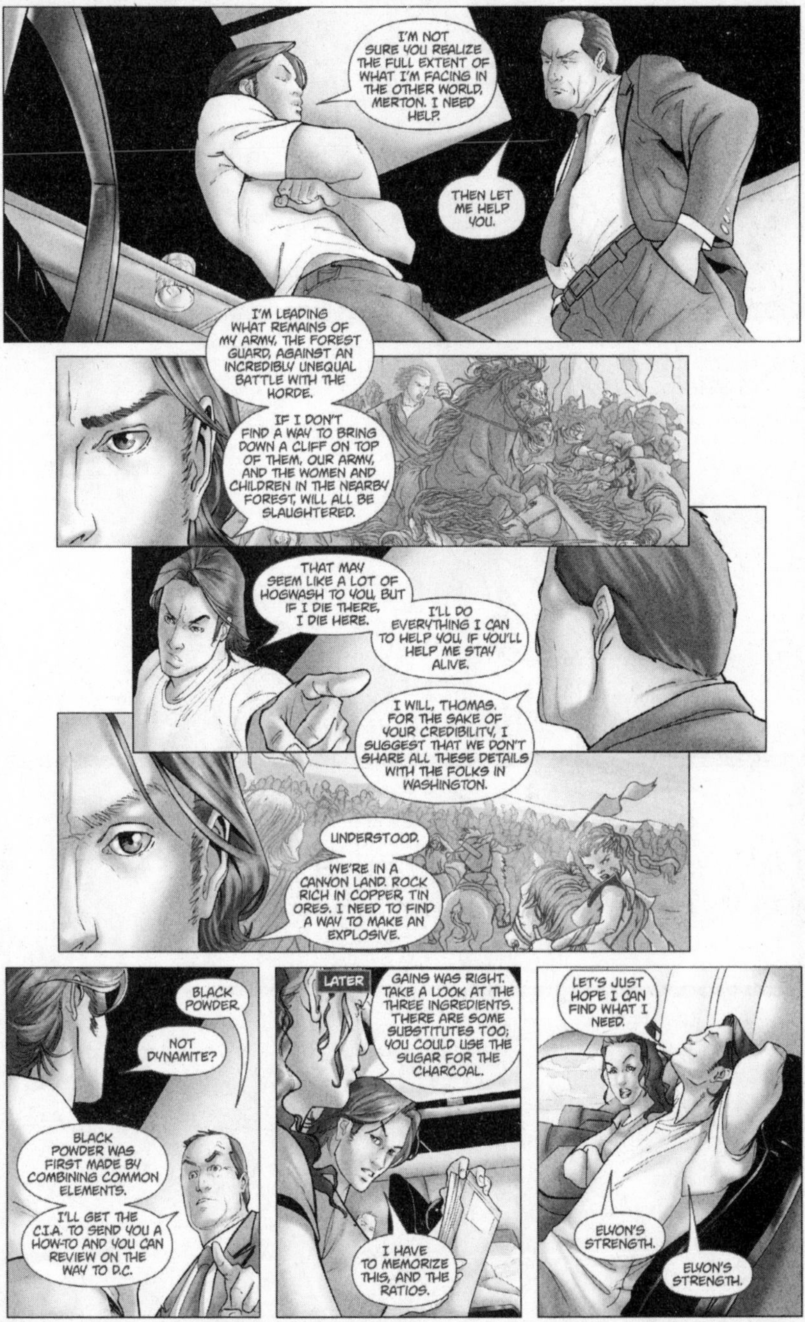
I'M NOT SURE YOU REALIZE THE FULL EXTENT OF WHAT I'M FACING IN THE OTHER WORLD, MERTON. I NEED HELP.
THEN LET ME HELP YOU.
I'M LEADING WHAT REMAINS OF MY ARMY, THE FOREST GUARD, AGAINST AN INCREDIBLY UNEQUAL BATTLE WITH THE HORDE.
IF I DON'T FIND A WAY TO BRING DOWN A CLIFF ON TOP OF THEM, OUR ARMY, AND THE WOMEN AND CHILDREN IN THE NEARBY FOREST, WILL ALL BE SLAUGHTERED.
THAT MAY SEEM LIKE A LOT OF HOGWASH TO YOU, BUT IF I DIE THERE, I DIE HERE.
I'LL DO EVERYTHING I CAN TO HELP YOU, IF YOU'LL HELP ME STAY ALIVE.
I WILL, THOMAS. FOR THE SAKE OF YOUR CREDIBILITY, I SUGGEST THAT WE DON'T SHARE ALL THESE DETAILS WITH THE FOLKS IN WASHINGTON.
UNDERSTOOD.
WE'RE IN A CANYON LAND. ROCK RICH IN COPPER, TIN ORES. I NEED TO FIND A WAY TO MAKE AN EXPLOSIVE.
BLACK POWDER.
NOT DYNAMITE?
BLACK POWDER WAS FIRST MADE BY COMBINING COMMON ELEMENTS.
I'LL GET THE C.I.A. TO SEND YOU A HOW-TO AND YOU CAN REVIEW ON THE WAY TO D.C.
LATER
GAINS WAS RIGHT. TAKE A LOOK AT THE THREE INGREDIENTS. THERE ARE SOME SUBSTITUTES TOO; YOU COULD USE THE SUGAR FOR THE CHARCOAL.
I HAVE TO MEMORIZE THIS, AND THE RATIOS.
LET'S JUST HOPE I CAN FIND WHAT I NEED.
ELYON'S STRENGTH.
ELYON'S STRENGTH.

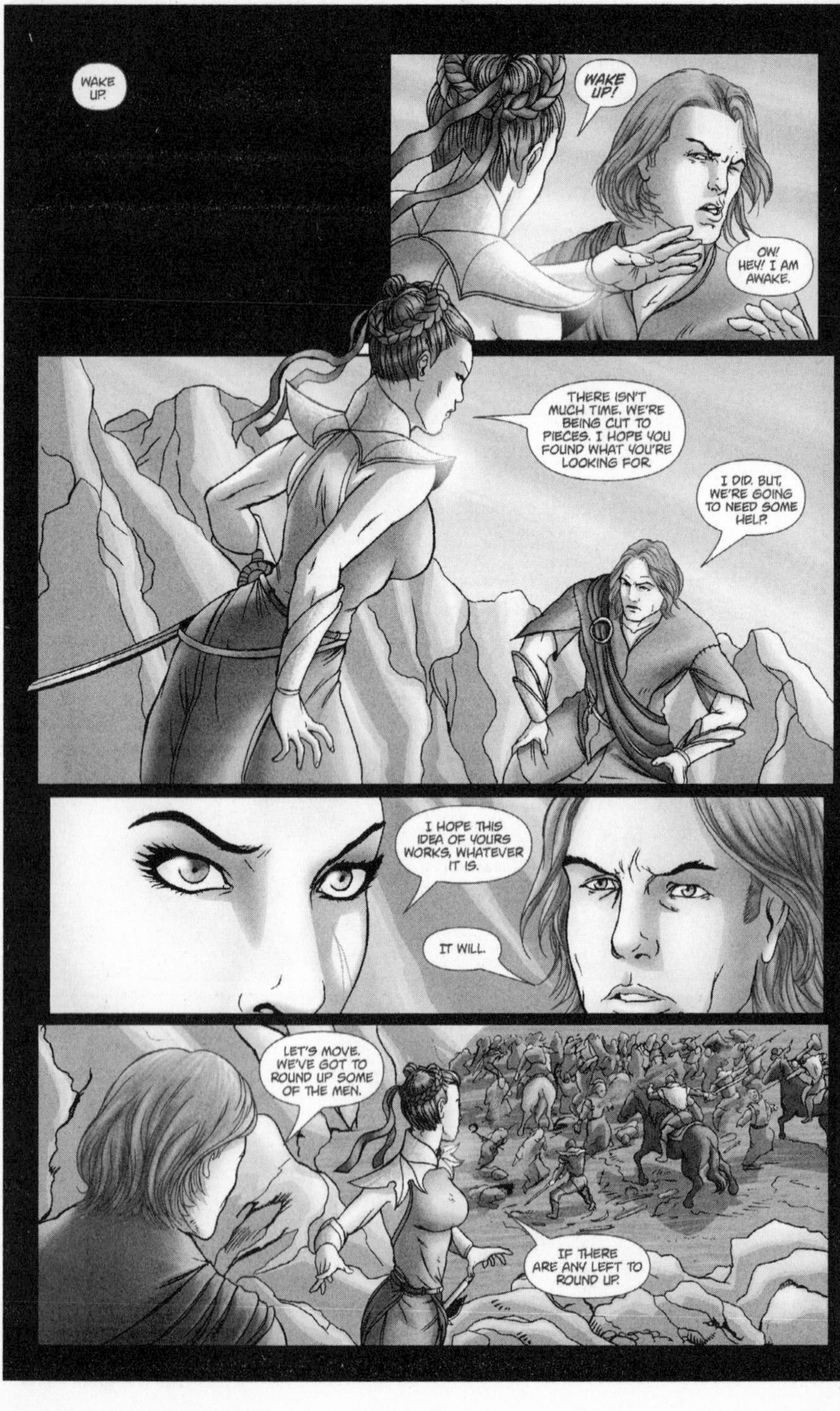
WAKE UP.
WAKE UP!
OW! HEY! I AM AWAKE.
THERE ISN'T MUCH TIME. WE'RE BEING CUT TO PIECES. I HOPE YOU FOUND WHAT YOU'RE LOOKING FOR.
I DID. BUT, WE'RE GOING TO NEED SOME HELP.
I HOPE THIS IDEA OF YOURS WORKS, WHATEVER IT IS.
IT WILL.
LET'S MOVE. WE'VE GOT TO ROUND UP SOME OF THE MEN.
IF THERE ARE ANY LEFT TO ROUND UP.

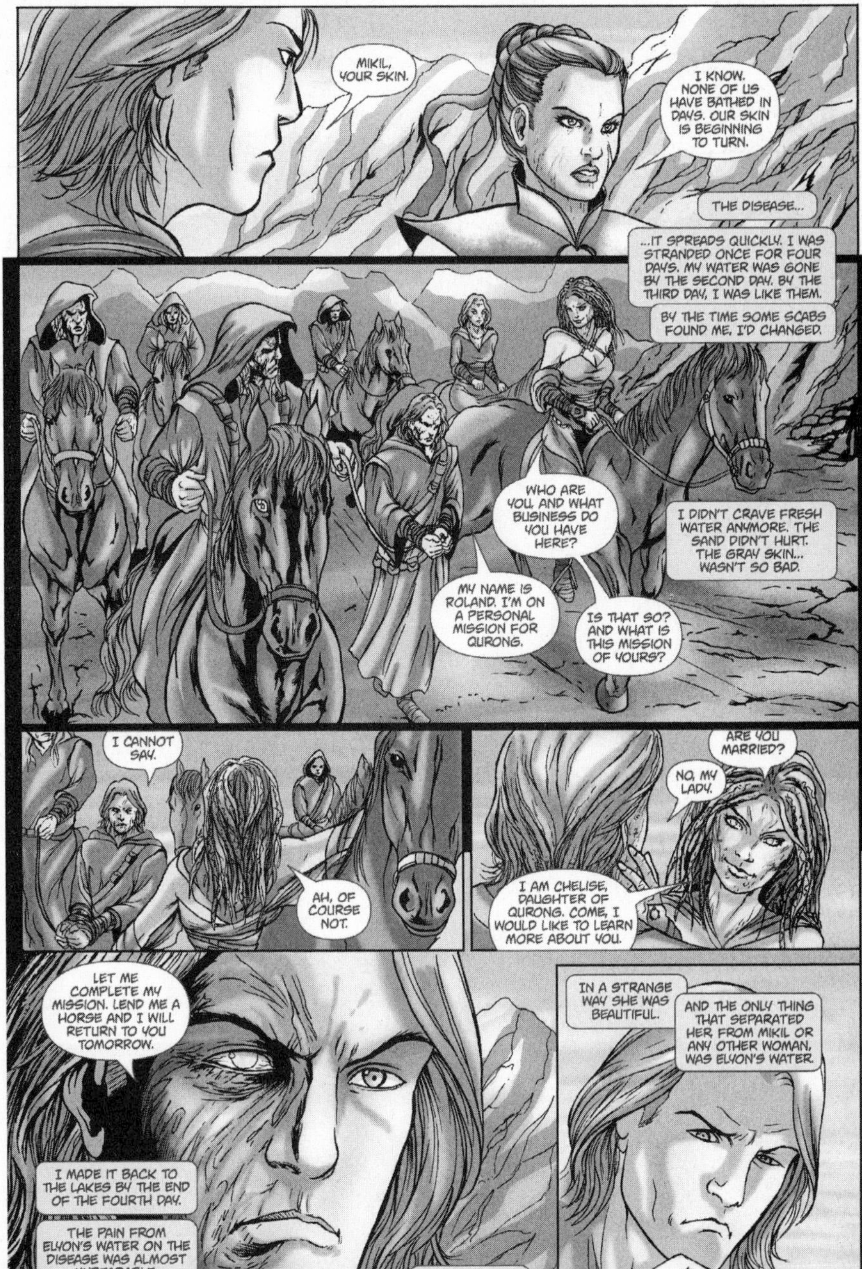
MIKIL, YOUR SKIN.
I KNOW. NONE OF US HAVE BATHED IN DAYS. OUR SKIN IS BEGINNING TO TURN.
THE DISEASE...
...IT SPREADS QUICKLY. I WAS STRANDED ONCE FOR FOUR DAYS. MY WATER WAS GONE BY THE SECOND DAY. BY THE THIRD DAY, I WAS LIKE THEM.
BY THE TIME SOME SCABS FOUND ME, I'D CHANGED.
WHO ARE YOU, AND WHAT BUSINESS DO YOU HAVE HERE?
MY NAME IS ROLAND. I'M ON A PERSONAL MISSION FOR QURONG.
IS THAT SO? AND WHAT IS THIS MISSION OF YOURS?
I DIDN'T CRAVE FRESH WATER ANYMORE. THE SAND DIDN'T HURT. THE GRAY SKIN... WASN'T SO BAD.
I CANNOT SAY.
AH, OF COURSE NOT.
ARE YOU MARRIED?
NO, MY LADY.
I AM CHELISE, DAUGHTER OF QURONG. COME, I WOULD LIKE TO LEARN MORE ABOUT YOU.
LET ME COMPLETE MY MISSION. LEND ME A HORSE AND I WILL RETURN TO YOU TOMORROW.
I MADE IT BACK TO THE LAKES BY THE END OF THE FOURTH DAY.
THE PAIN FROM ELYON'S WATER ON THE DISEASE WAS ALMOST UNBEARABLE.
THE DISEASE WASHED AWAY, BUT THE MEMORY OF CHELISE REMAINED.
THE DAUGHTER OF THE MIGHTY QURONG.
IN A STRANGE WAY SHE WAS BEAUTIFUL.
AND THE ONLY THING THAT SEPARATED HER FROM MIKIL OR ANY OTHER WOMAN, WAS ELYON'S WATER.

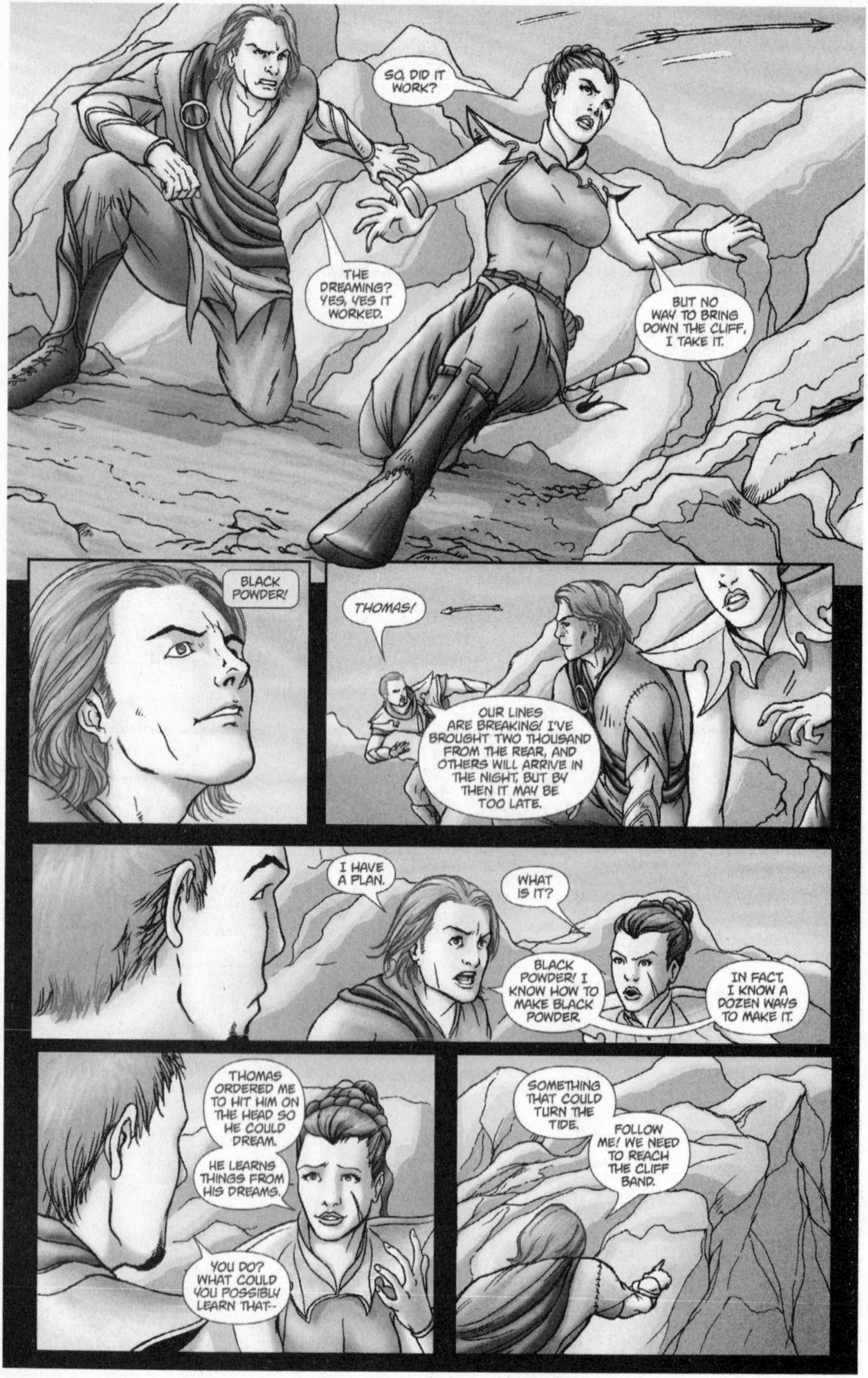
SO, DID IT WORK?
THE DREAMING? YES, YES IT WORKED.
BUT NO WAY TO BRING DOWN THE CLIFF, I TAKE IT.
BLACK POWDER!
THOMAS!
OUR LINES ARE BREAKING! I'VE BROUGHT TWO THOUSAND FROM THE REAR, AND OTHERS WILL ARRIVE IN THE NIGHT, BUT BY THEN IT MAY BE TOO LATE.
I HAVE A PLAN.
WHAT IS IT?
BLACK POWDER! I KNOW HOW TO MAKE BLACK POWDER.
IN FACT, I KNOW A DOZEN WAYS TO MAKE IT.
THOMAS ORDERED ME TO HIT HIM ON THE HEAD SO HE COULD DREAM.
HE LEARNS THINGS FROM HIS DREAMS.
YOU DO? WHAT COULD YOU POSSIBLY LEARN THAT-
SOMETHING THAT COULD TURN THE TIDE.
FOLLOW ME! WE NEED TO REACH THE CLIFF BAND.

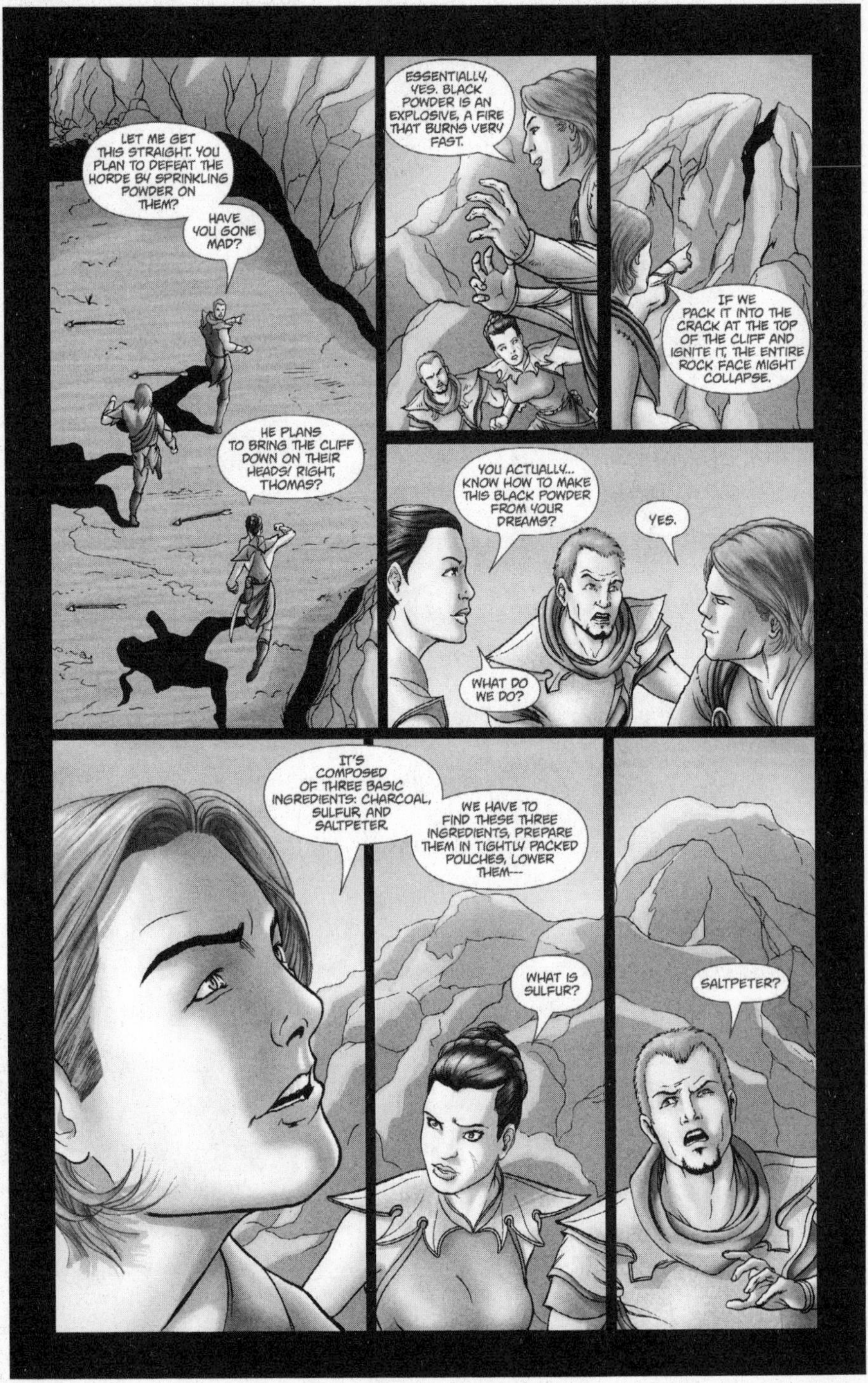
LET ME GET THIS STRAIGHT. YOU PLAN TO DEFEAT THE HORDE BY SPRINKLING POWDER ON THEM?
HAVE YOU GONE MAD?
HE PLANS TO BRING THE CLIFF DOWN ON THEIR HEADS! RIGHT, THOMAS?
ESSENTIALLY, YES. BLACK POWDER IS AN EXPLOSIVE, A FIRE THAT BURNS VERY FAST.
IF WE PACK IT INTO THE CRACK AT THE TOP OF THE CLIFF AND IGNITE IT, THE ENTIRE ROCK FACE MIGHT COLLAPSE.
YOU ACTUALLY... KNOW HOW TO MAKE THIS BLACK POWDER FROM YOUR DREAMS?
YES.
WHAT DO WE DO?
IT'S COMPOSED OF THREE BASIC INGREDIENTS: CHARCOAL, SULFUR AND SALTPETER.
WE HAVE TO FIND THESE THREE INGREDIENTS, PREPARE THEM IN TIGHTLY PACKED POUCHES, LOWER THEM---
WHAT IS SULFUR?
SALTPETER?

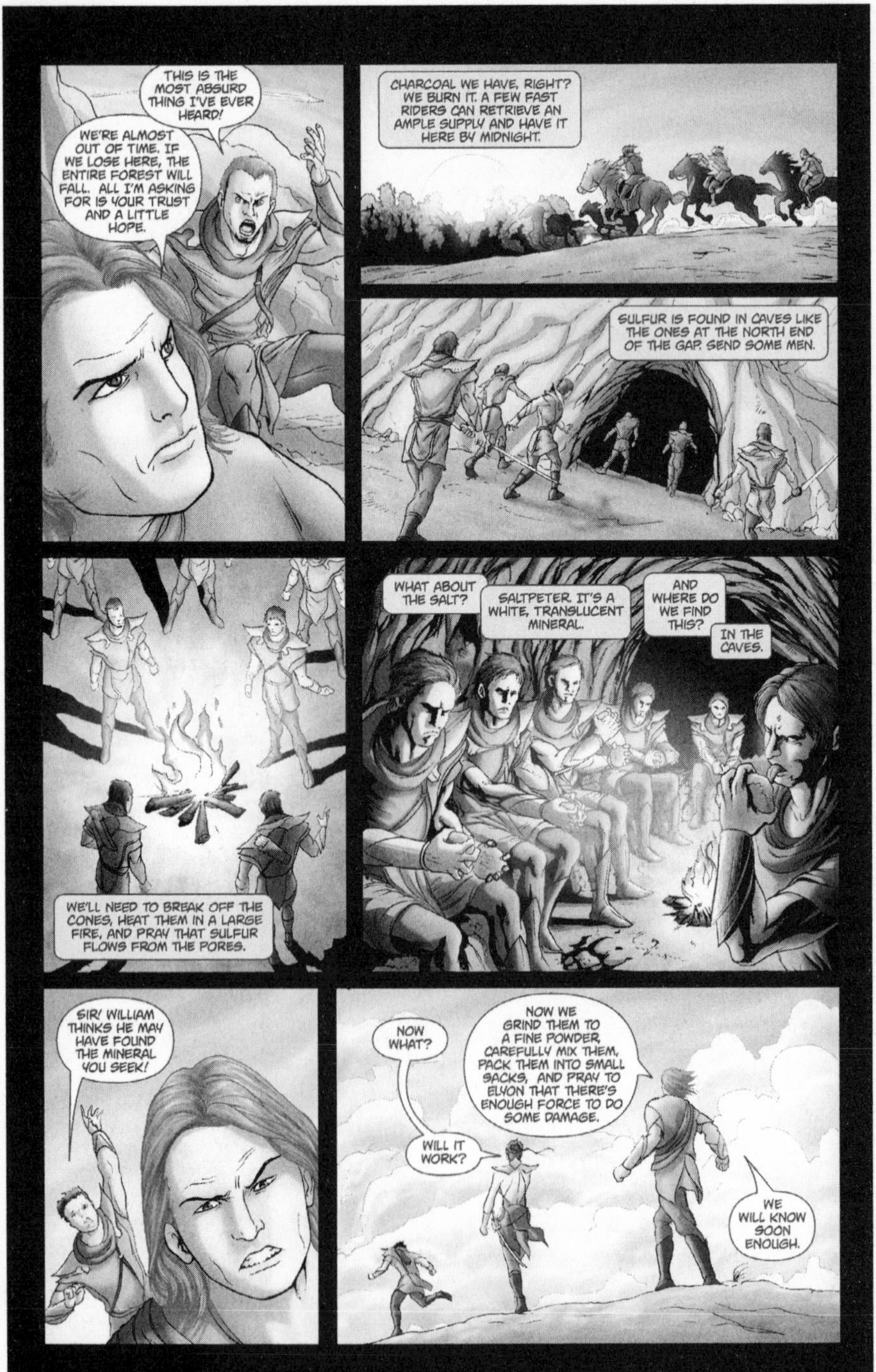
THIS IS THE MOST ABSURD THING I'VE EVER HEARD!
WE'RE ALMOST OUT OF TIME. IF WE LOSE HERE, THE ENTIRE FOREST WILL FALL. ALL I'M ASKING FOR IS YOUR TRUST AND A LITTLE HOPE.
CHARCOAL WE HAVE, RIGHT? WE BURN IT. A FEW FAST RIDERS CAN RETRIEVE AN AMPLE SUPPLY AND HAVE IT HERE BY MIDNIGHT.
SULFUR IS FOUND IN CAVES LIKE THE ONES AT THE NORTH END OF THE GAP. SEND SOME MEN.
WE'LL NEED TO BREAK OFF THE CONES, HEAT THEM IN A LARGE FIRE, AND PRAY THAT SULFUR FLOWS FROM THE PORES.
WHAT ABOUT THE SALT?
SALTPETER. IT'S A WHITE, TRANSLUCENT MINERAL.
AND WHERE DO WE FIND THIS?
IN THE CAVES.
SIR! WILLIAM THINKS HE MAY HAVE FOUND THE MINERAL YOU SEEK!
NOW WHAT?
NOW WE GRIND THEM TO A FINE POWDER, CAREFULLY MIX THEM, PACK THEM INTO SMALL SACKS, AND PRAY TO ELYON THAT THERE'S ENOUGH FORCE TO DO SOME DAMAGE.
WILL IT WORK?
WE WILL KNOW SOON ENOUGH.

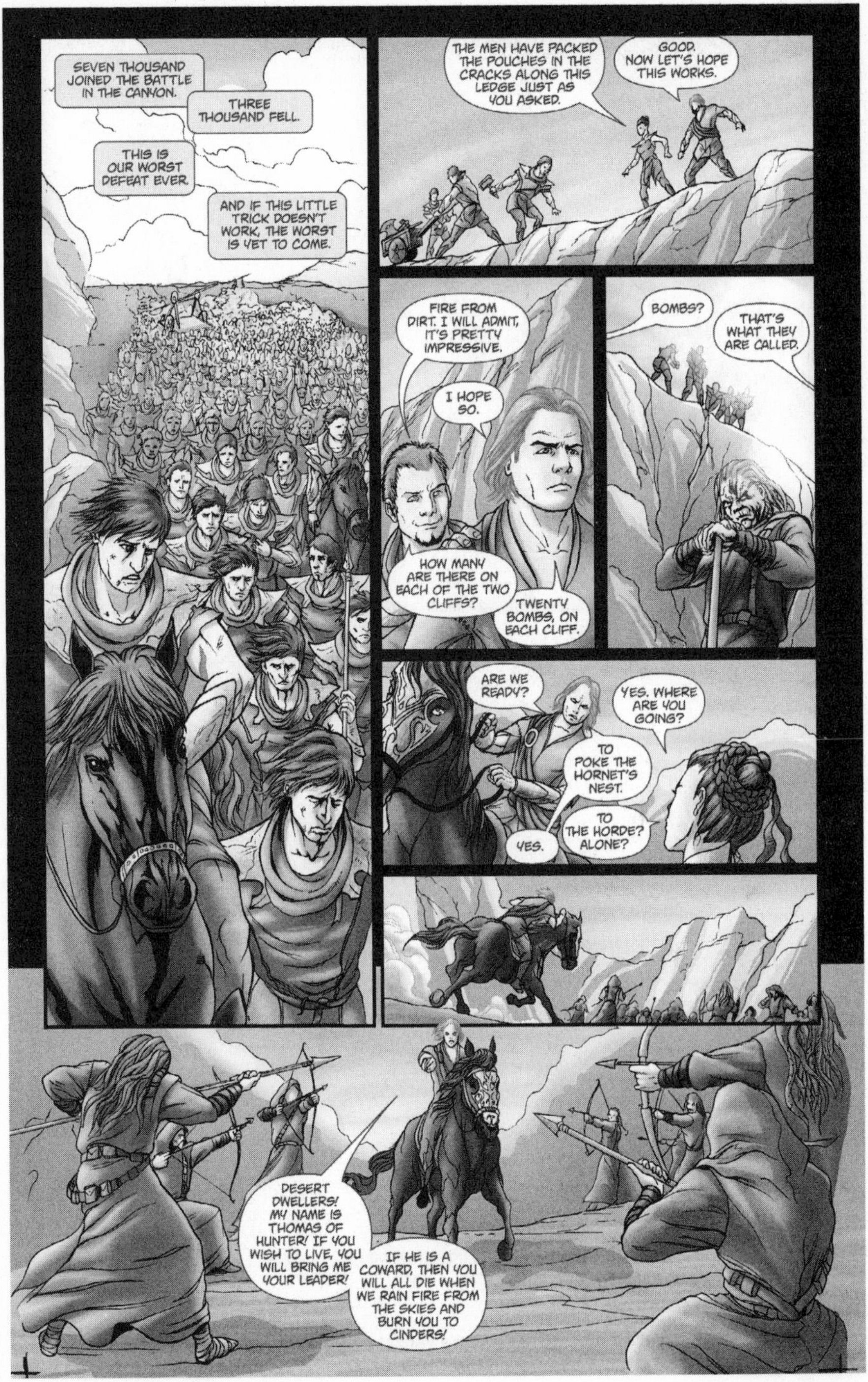
SEVEN THOUSAND JOINED THE BATTLE IN THE CANYON.
THREE THOUSAND FELL.
THIS IS OUR WORST DEFEAT EVER.
AND IF THIS LITTLE TRICK DOESN'T WORK, THE WORST IS YET TO COME.
THE MEN HAVE PACKED THE POUCHES IN THE CRACKS ALONG THIS LEDGE JUST AS YOU ASKED.
GOOD. NOW LET'S HOPE THIS WORKS.
FIRE FROM DIRT. I WILL ADMIT, IT'S PRETTY IMPRESSIVE.
I HOPE SO.
HOW MANY ARE THERE ON EACH OF THE TWO CLIFFS?
TWENTY BOMBS, ON EACH CLIFF.
BOMBS?
THAT'S WHAT THEY ARE CALLED.
ARE WE READY?
YES. WHERE ARE YOU GOING?
TO POKE THE HORNET'S NEST.
TO THE HORDE? ALONE?
YES.
DESERT DWELLERS! MY NAME IS THOMAS OF HUNTER! IF YOU WISH TO LIVE, YOU WILL BRING ME YOUR LEADER!
IF HE IS A COWARD, THEN YOU WILL ALL DIE WHEN WE RAIN FIRE FROM THE SKIES AND BURN YOU TO CINDERS!

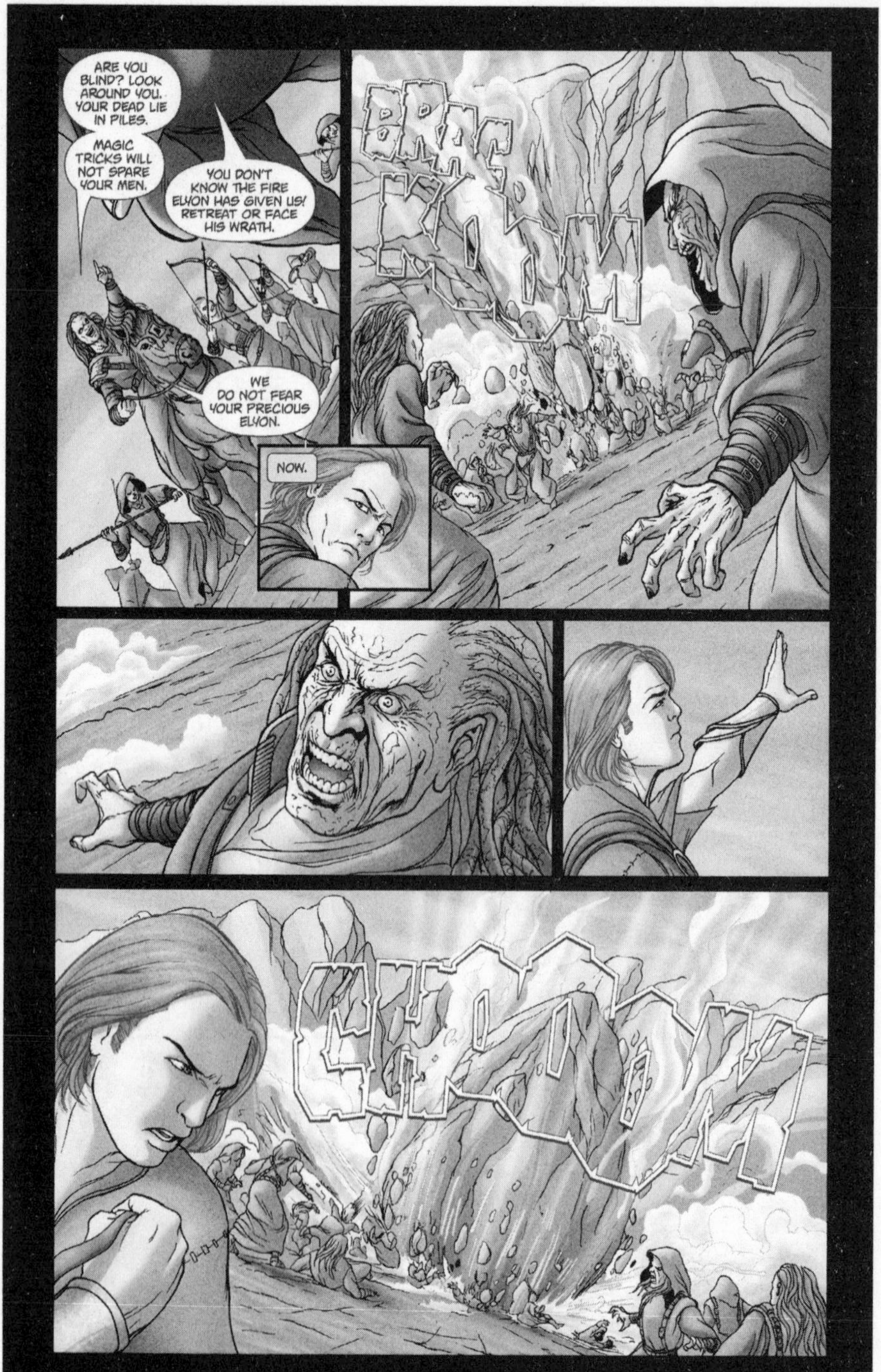

ARE YOU BLIND? LOOK AROUND YOU. YOUR DEAD LIE IN PILES.
MAGIC TRICKS WILL NOT SPARE YOUR MEN.
YOU DON'T KNOW THE FIRE ELYON HAS GIVEN US! RETREAT OR FACE HIS WRATH.
WE DO NOT FEAR YOUR PRECIOUS ELYON.
NOW.

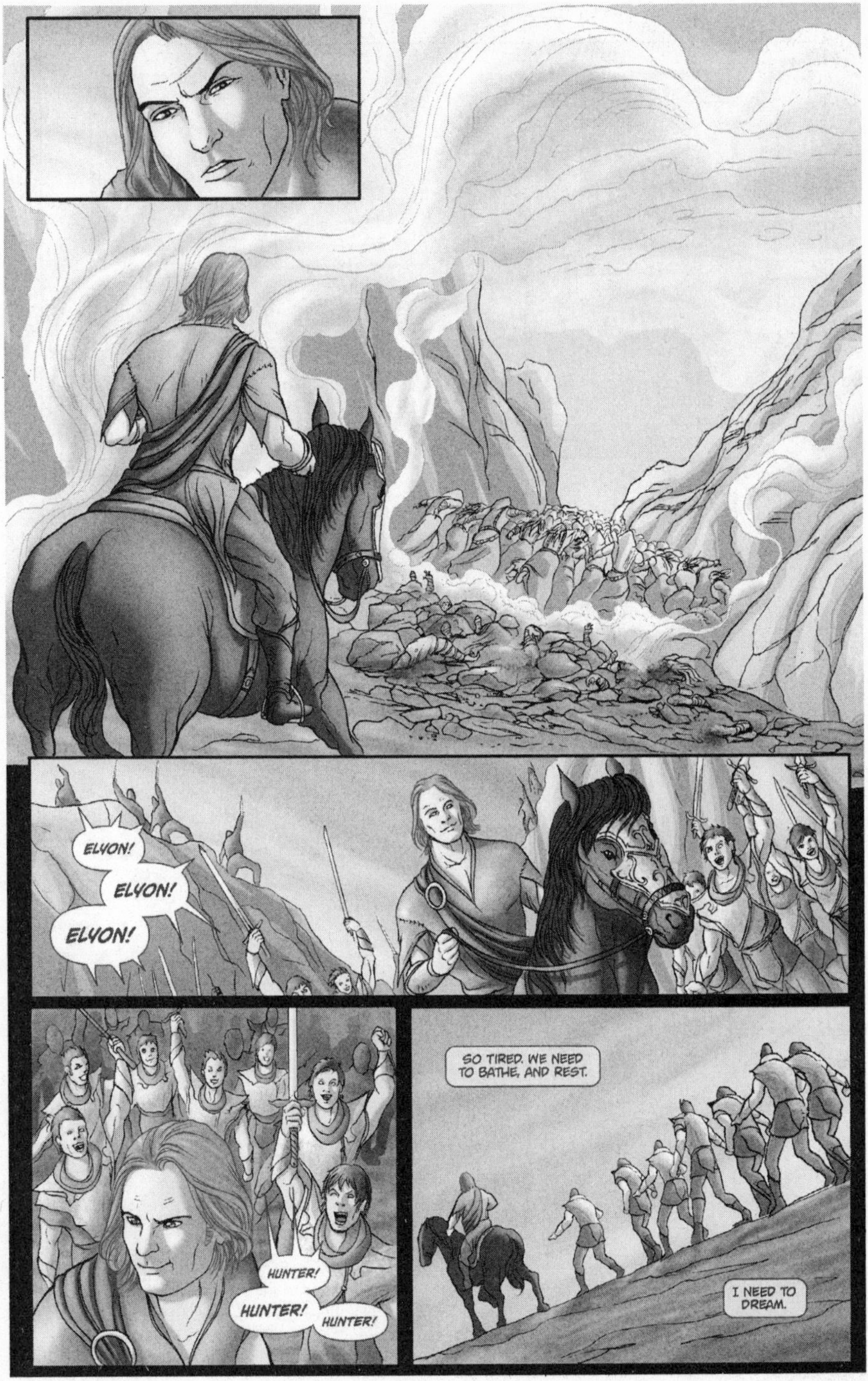
ELYON!
ELYON!
ELYON!
HUNTER!
HUNTER!
HUNTER!
SO TIRED. WE NEED TO BATHE, AND REST.
I NEED TO DREAM.

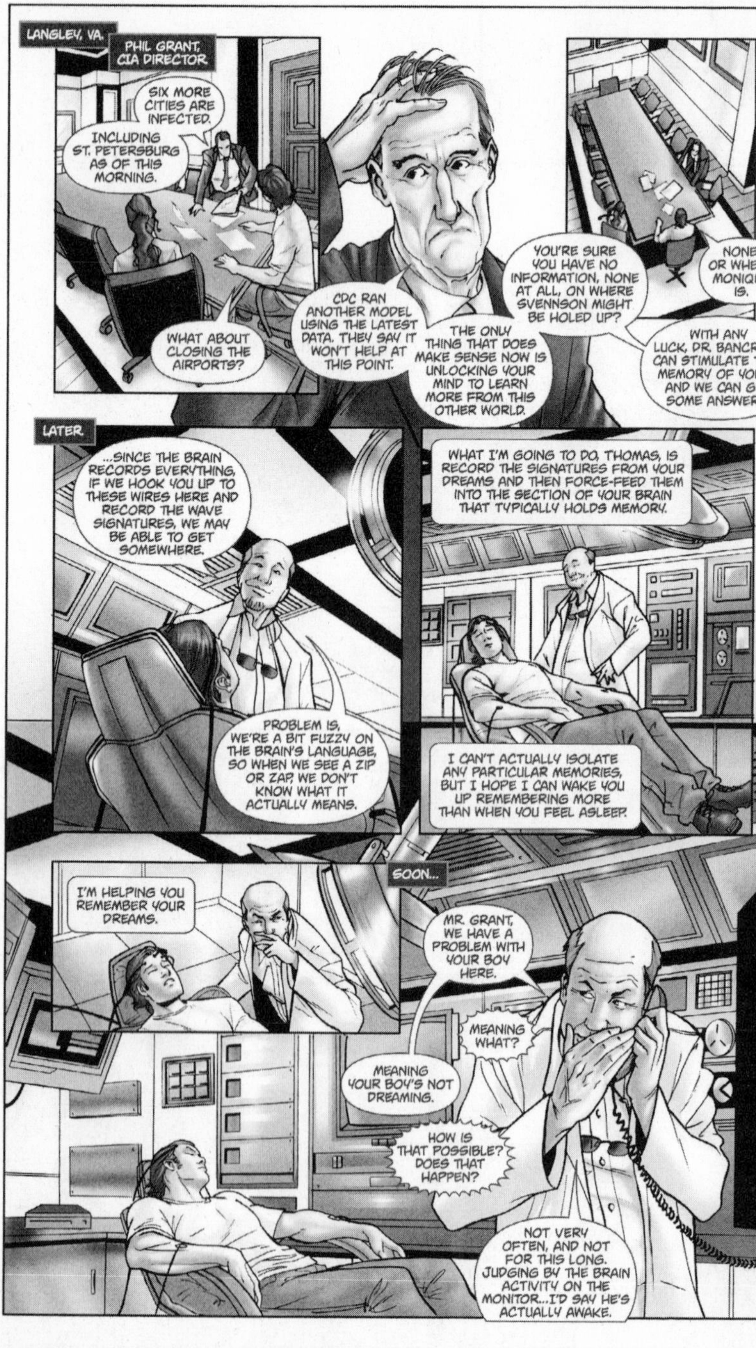
LANGLEY, VA.
PHIL GRANT, CIA DIRECTOR
SIX MORE CITIES ARE INFECTED.
INCLUDING ST. PETERSBURG AS OF THIS MORNING.
WHAT ABOUT CLOSING THE AIRPORTS?
CDC RAN ANOTHER MODEL USING THE LATEST DATA. THEY SAY IT WON'T HELP AT THIS POINT.
THE ONLY THING THAT DOES MAKE SENSE NOW IS UNLOCKING YOUR MIND TO LEARN MORE FROM THIS OTHER WORLD.
YOU'RE SURE YOU HAVE NO INFORMATION, NONE AT ALL, ON WHERE SVENNSON MIGHT BE HOLED UP?
NONE. OR WHERE MONIQUE IS.
WITH ANY LUCK, DR. BANCROFT CAN STIMULATE THAT MEMORY OF YOURS AND WE CAN GET SOME ANSWERS.
LATER
...SINCE THE BRAIN RECORDS EVERYTHING, IF WE HOOK YOU UP TO THESE WIRES HERE AND RECORD THE WAVE SIGNATURES, WE MAY BE ABLE TO GET SOMEWHERE.
PROBLEM IS, WE'RE A BIT FUZZY ON THE BRAIN'S LANGUAGE, SO WHEN WE SEE A ZIP OR ZAP, WE DON'T KNOW WHAT IT ACTUALLY MEANS.
WHAT I'M GOING TO DO, THOMAS, IS RECORD THE SIGNATURES FROM YOUR DREAMS AND THEN FORCE-FEED THEM INTO THE SECTION OF YOUR BRAIN THAT TYPICALLY HOLDS MEMORY.
I CAN'T ACTUALLY ISOLATE ANY PARTICULAR MEMORIES, BUT I HOPE I CAN WAKE YOU UP REMEMBERING MORE THAN WHEN YOU FEEL ASLEEP.
I'M HELPING YOU REMEMBER YOUR DREAMS.
SOON...
MR. GRANT, WE HAVE A PROBLEM WITH YOUR BOY HERE.
MEANING WHAT?
MEANING YOUR BOY'S NOT DREAMING.
HOW IS THAT POSSIBLE? DOES THAT HAPPEN?
NOT VERY OFTEN, AND NOT FOR THIS LONG. JUDGING BY THE BRAIN ACTIVITY ON THE MONITOR...I'D SAY HE'S ACTUALLY AWAKE.

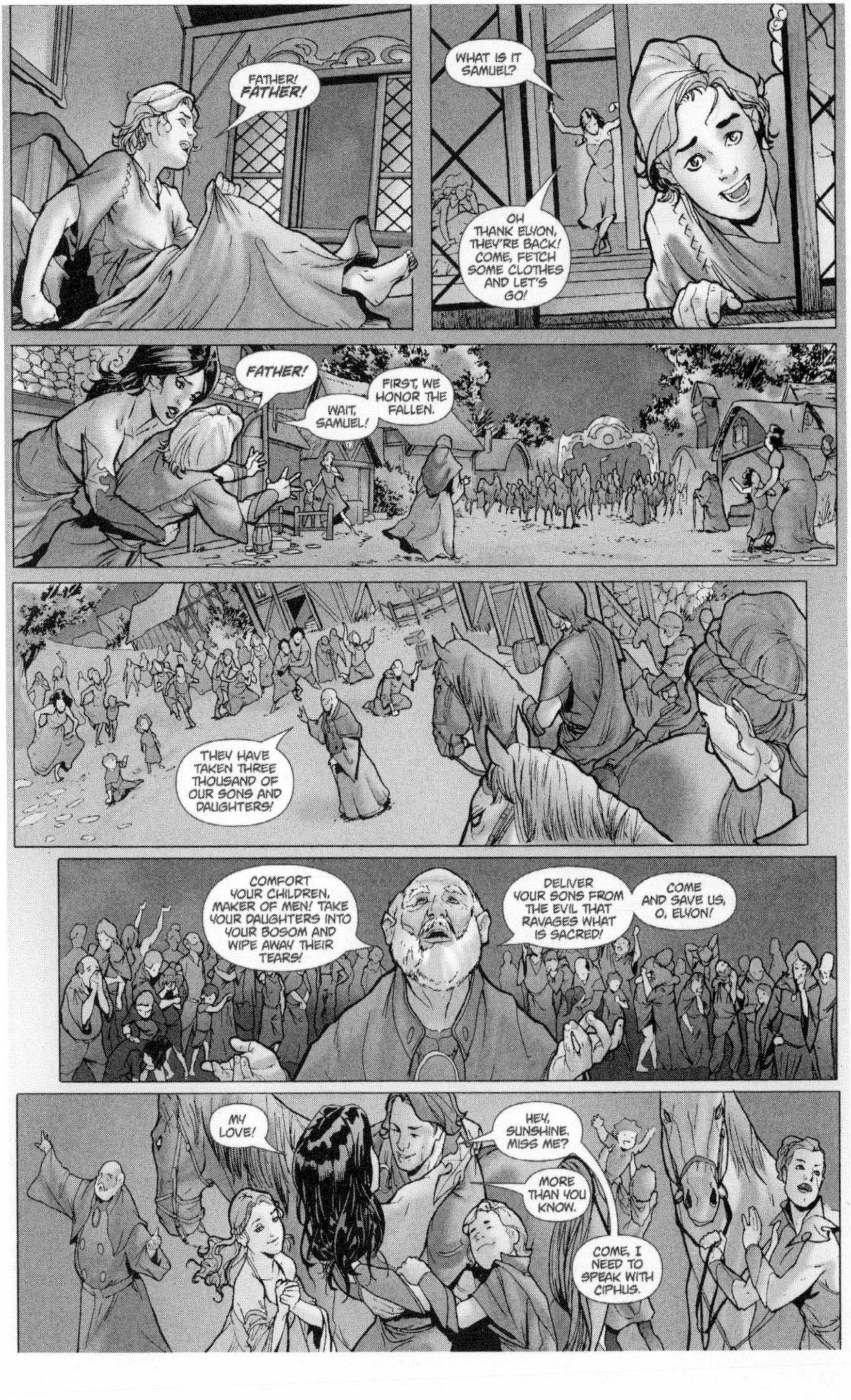

FATHER! FATHER!
WHAT IS IT SAMUEL?
OH THANK ELYON, THEY'RE BACK! COME, FETCH SOME CLOTHES AND LET'S GO!
FATHER!
WAIT, SAMUEL!
FIRST, WE HONOR THE FALLEN.
THEY HAVE TAKEN THREE THOUSAND OF OUR SONS AND DAUGHTERS!
COMFORT YOUR CHILDREN, MAKER OF MEN! TAKE YOUR DAUGHTERS INTO YOUR BOSOM AND WIPE AWAY THEIR TEARS!
DELIVER YOUR SONS FROM THE EVIL THAT RAVAGES WHAT IS SACRED!
COME AND SAVE US, O, ELYON!
MY LOVE!
HEY, SUNSHINE, MISS ME?
MORE THAN YOU KNOW.
COME, I NEED TO SPEAK WITH CIPHUS.

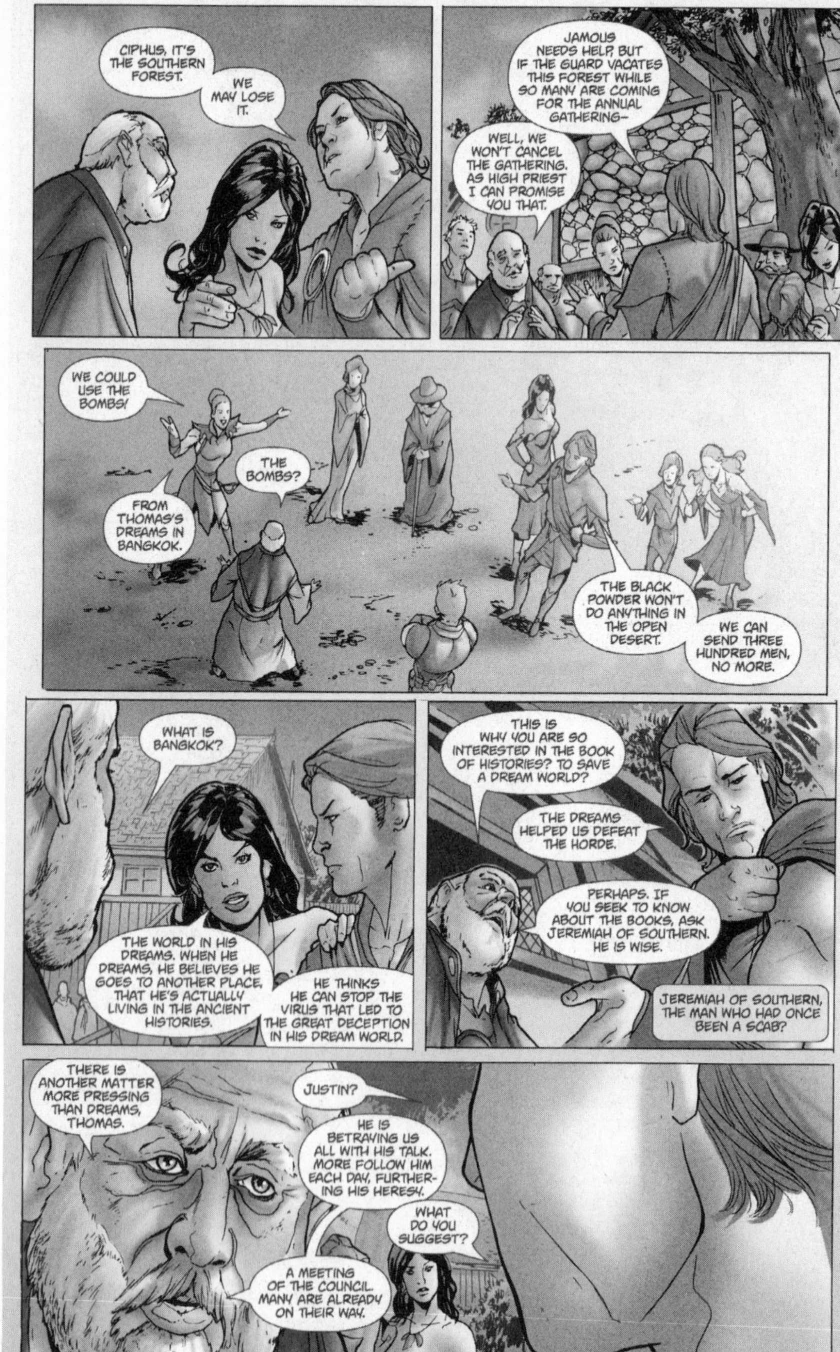

CIPHUS, IT'S THE SOUTHERN FOREST.
WE MAY LOSE IT.
JAMOUS NEEDS HELP, BUT IF THE GUARD VACATES THIS FOREST WHILE SO MANY ARE COMING FOR THE ANNUAL GATHERING—
WELL, WE WON'T CANCEL THE GATHERING. AS HIGH PRIEST I CAN PROMISE YOU THAT.
WE COULD USE THE BOMBS!
THE BOMBS?
FROM THOMAS'S DREAMS IN BANGKOK.
THE BLACK POWDER WON'T DO ANYTHING IN THE OPEN DESERT.
WE CAN SEND THREE HUNDRED MEN, NO MORE.
WHAT IS BANGKOK?
THE WORLD IN HIS DREAMS. WHEN HE DREAMS, HE BELIEVES HE GOES TO ANOTHER PLACE, THAT HE'S ACTUALLY LIVING IN THE ANCIENT HISTORIES.
HE THINKS HE CAN STOP THE VIRUS THAT LED TO THE GREAT DECEPTION IN HIS DREAM WORLD.
THIS IS WHY YOU ARE SO INTERESTED IN THE BOOK OF HISTORIES? TO SAVE A DREAM WORLD?
THE DREAMS HELPED US DEFEAT THE HORDE.
PERHAPS. IF YOU SEEK TO KNOW ABOUT THE BOOKS, ASK JEREMIAH OF SOUTHERN. HE IS WISE.
JEREMIAH OF SOUTHERN, THE MAN WHO HAD ONCE BEEN A SCAB?
THERE IS ANOTHER MATTER MORE PRESSING THAN DREAMS, THOMAS.
JUSTIN?
HE IS BETRAYING US ALL WITH HIS TALK. MORE FOLLOW HIM EACH DAY, FURTHERING HIS HERESY.
WHAT DO YOU SUGGEST?
A MEETING OF THE COUNCIL. MANY ARE ALREADY ON THEIR WAY.

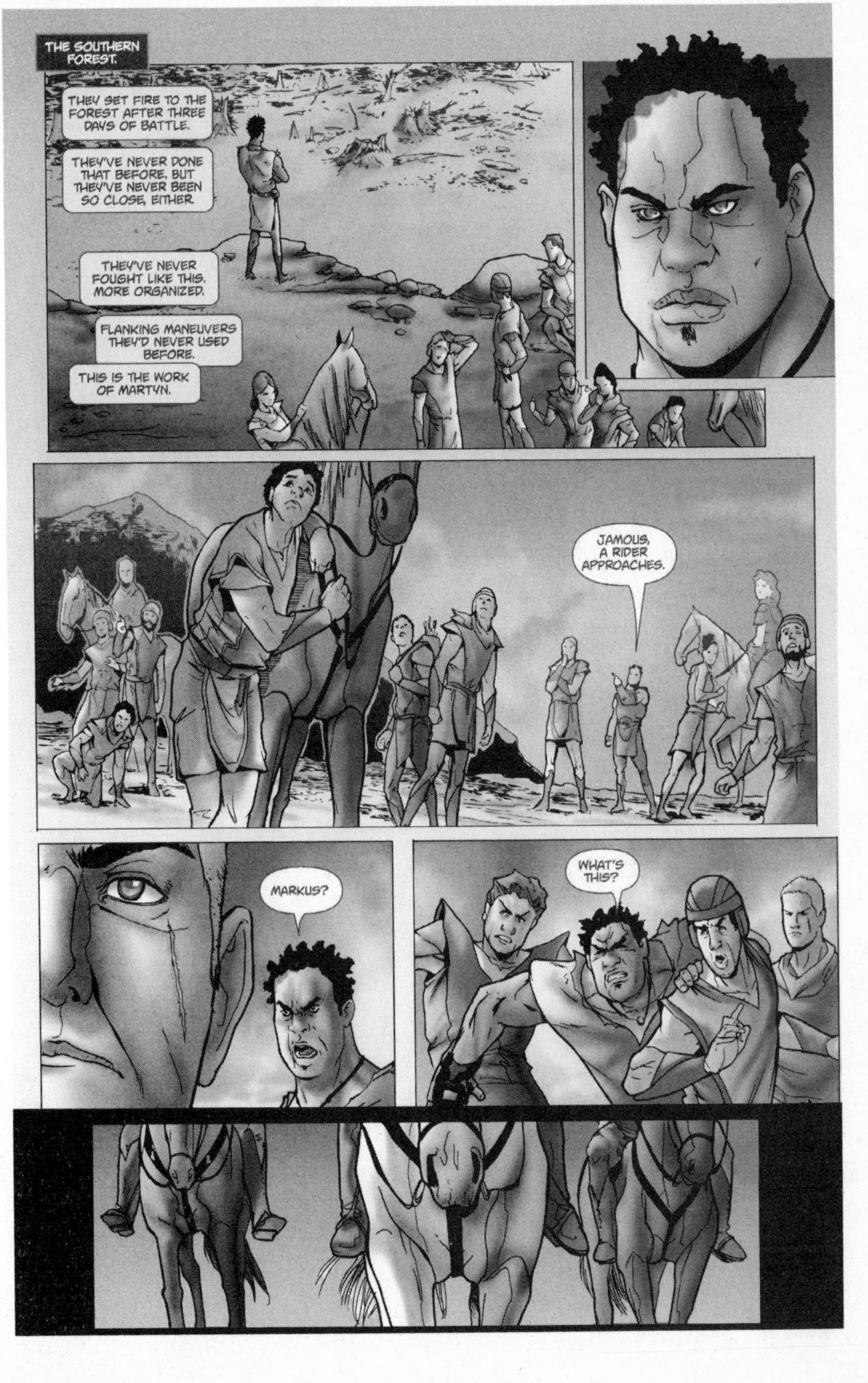
THE SOUTHERN FOREST.
THEY SET FIRE TO THE FOREST AFTER THREE DAYS OF BATTLE.
THEY'VE NEVER DONE THAT BEFORE. BUT THEY'VE NEVER BEEN SO CLOSE, EITHER.
THEY'VE NEVER FOUGHT LIKE THIS. MORE ORGANIZED.
FLANKING MANEUVERS THEY'D NEVER USED BEFORE.
THIS IS THE WORK OF MARTYN.
JAMOUS, A RIDER APPROACHES.
MARKUS?
WHAT'S THIS?

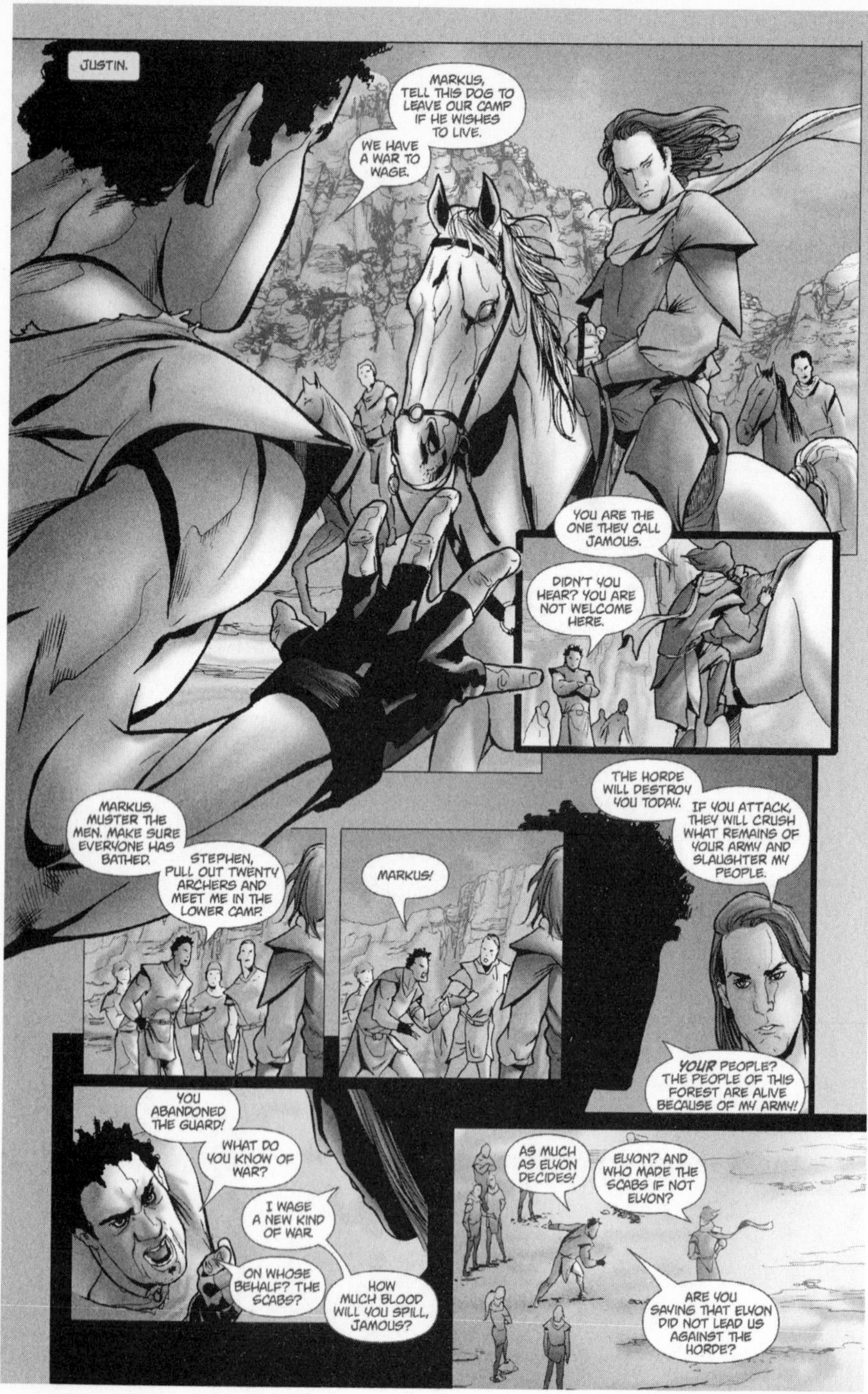
JUSTIN.
MARKUS, TELL THIS DOG TO LEAVE OUR CAMP IF HE WISHES TO LIVE.
WE HAVE A WAR TO WAGE.
YOU ARE THE ONE THEY CALL JAMOUS.
DIDN'T YOU HEAR? YOU ARE NOT WELCOME HERE.
MARKUS, MUSTER THE MEN. MAKE SURE EVERYONE HAS BATHED.
STEPHEN, PULL OUT TWENTY ARCHERS AND MEET ME IN THE LOWER CAMP.
MARKUS!
THE HORDE WILL DESTROY YOU TODAY.
IF YOU ATTACK, THEY WILL CRUSH WHAT REMAINS OF YOUR ARMY AND SLAUGHTER MY PEOPLE.
YOUR PEOPLE? THE PEOPLE OF THIS FOREST ARE ALIVE BECAUSE OF MY ARMY!
YOU ABANDONED THE GUARD!
WHAT DO YOU KNOW OF WAR?
I WAGE A NEW KIND OF WAR.
ON WHOSE BEHALF? THE SCABS?
HOW MUCH BLOOD WILL YOU SPILL, JAMOUS?
AS MUCH AS ELYON DECIDES!
ELYON? AND WHO MADE THE SCABS IF NOT ELYON?
ARE YOU SAYING THAT ELYON DID NOT LEAD US AGAINST THE HORDE?

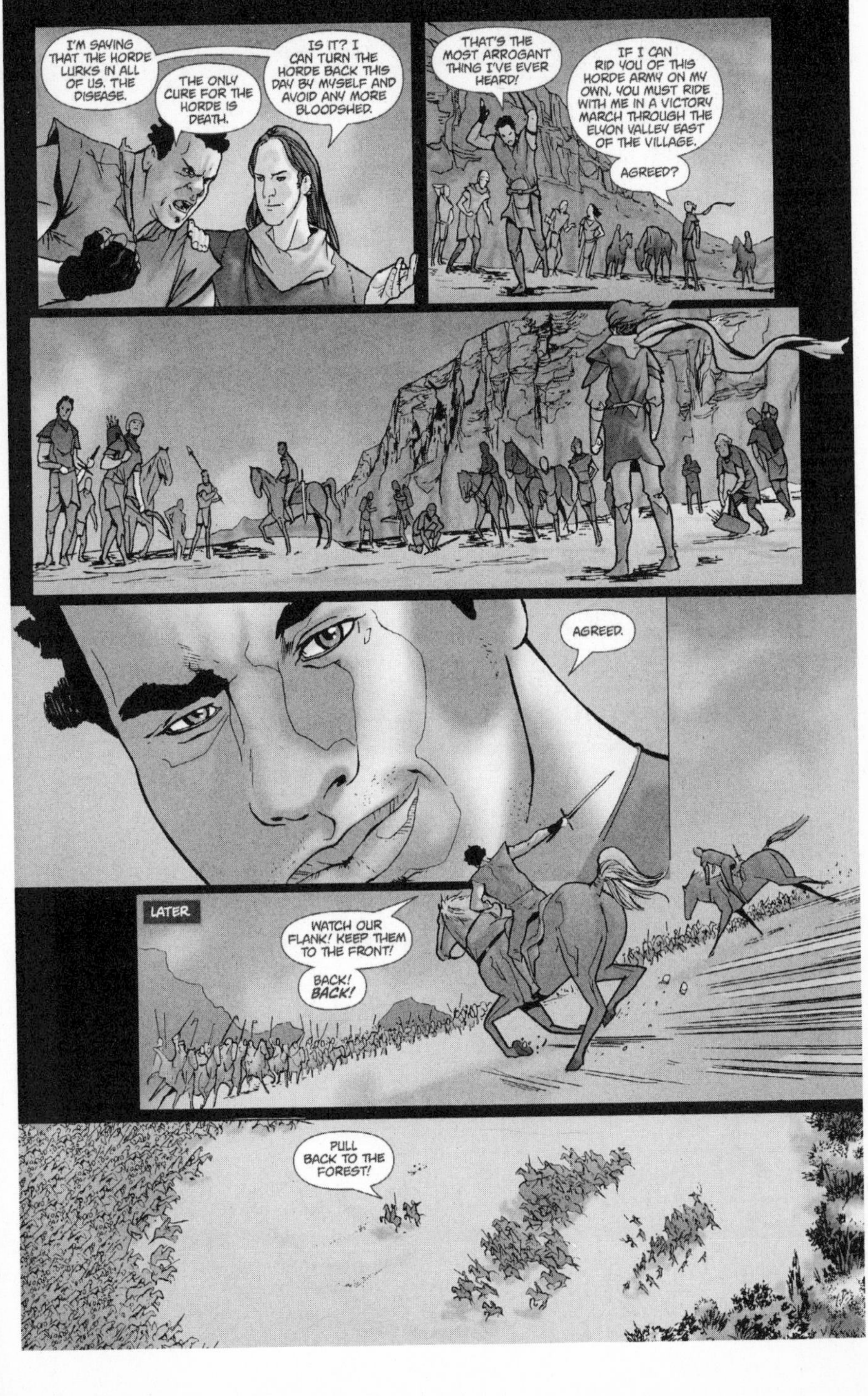
I'M SAYING THAT THE HORDE LURKS IN ALL OF US. THE DISEASE.
IS IT? I CAN TURN THE HORDE BACK THIS DAY BY MYSELF AND AVOID ANY MORE BLOODSHED.
THE ONLY CURE FOR THE HORDE IS DEATH.
THAT'S THE MOST ARROGANT THING I'VE EVER HEARD!
IF I CAN RID YOU OF THIS HORDE ARMY ON MY OWN, YOU MUST RIDE WITH ME IN A VICTORY MARCH THROUGH THE ELYON VALLEY EAST OF THE VILLAGE.
AGREED?
AGREED.
LATER
WATCH OUR FLANK! KEEP THEM TO THE FRONT!
BACK! BACK!
PULL BACK TO THE FOREST!

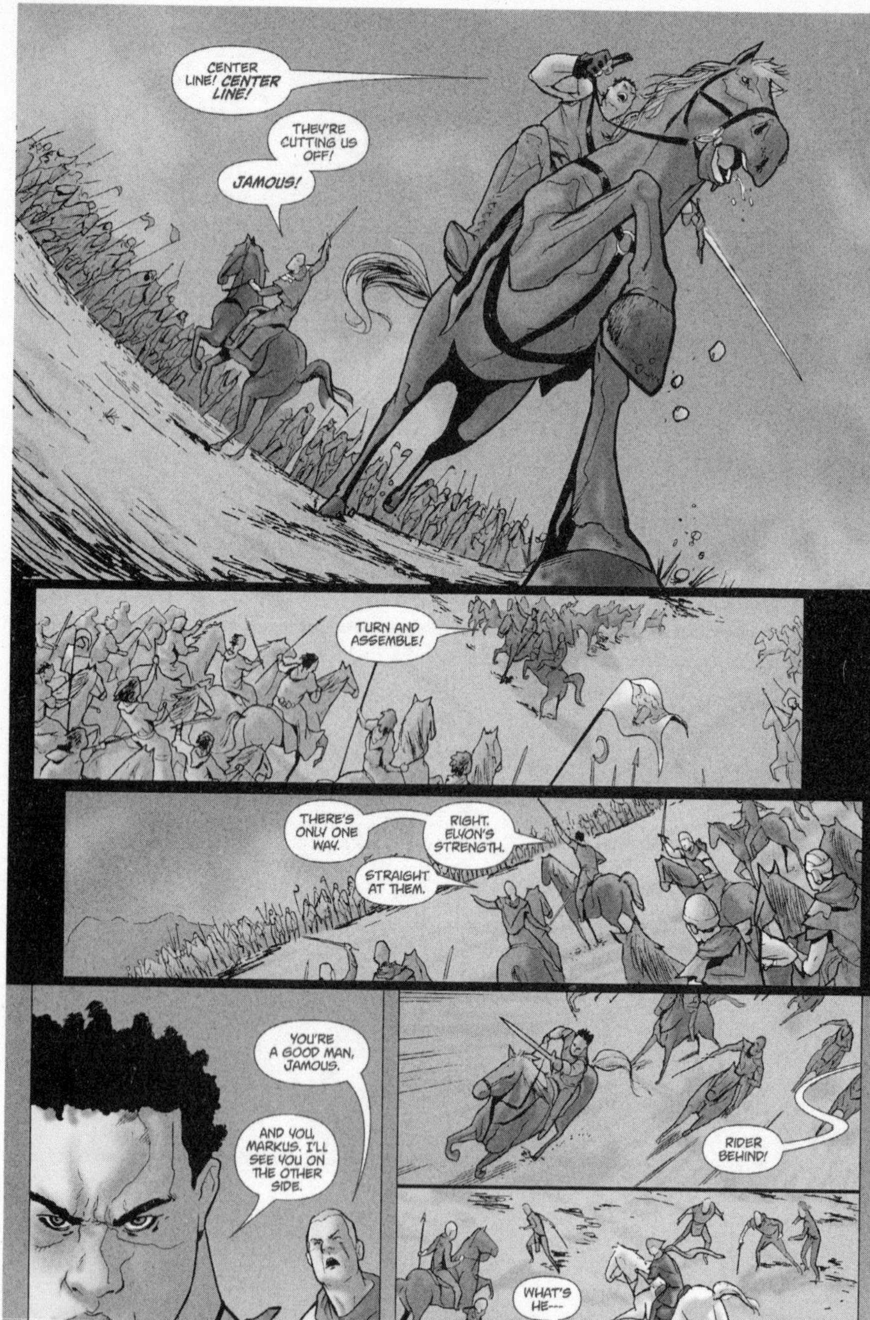
CENTER LINE! CENTER LINE!
THEY'RE CUTTING US OFF!
JAMOUS!
TURN AND ASSEMBLE!
THERE'S ONLY ONE WAY.
RIGHT. ELYON'S STRENGTH.
STRAIGHT AT THEM.
YOU'RE A GOOD MAN, JAMOUS.
AND YOU, MARKUS. I'LL SEE YOU ON THE OTHER SIDE.
RIDER BEHIND!
WHAT'S HE---

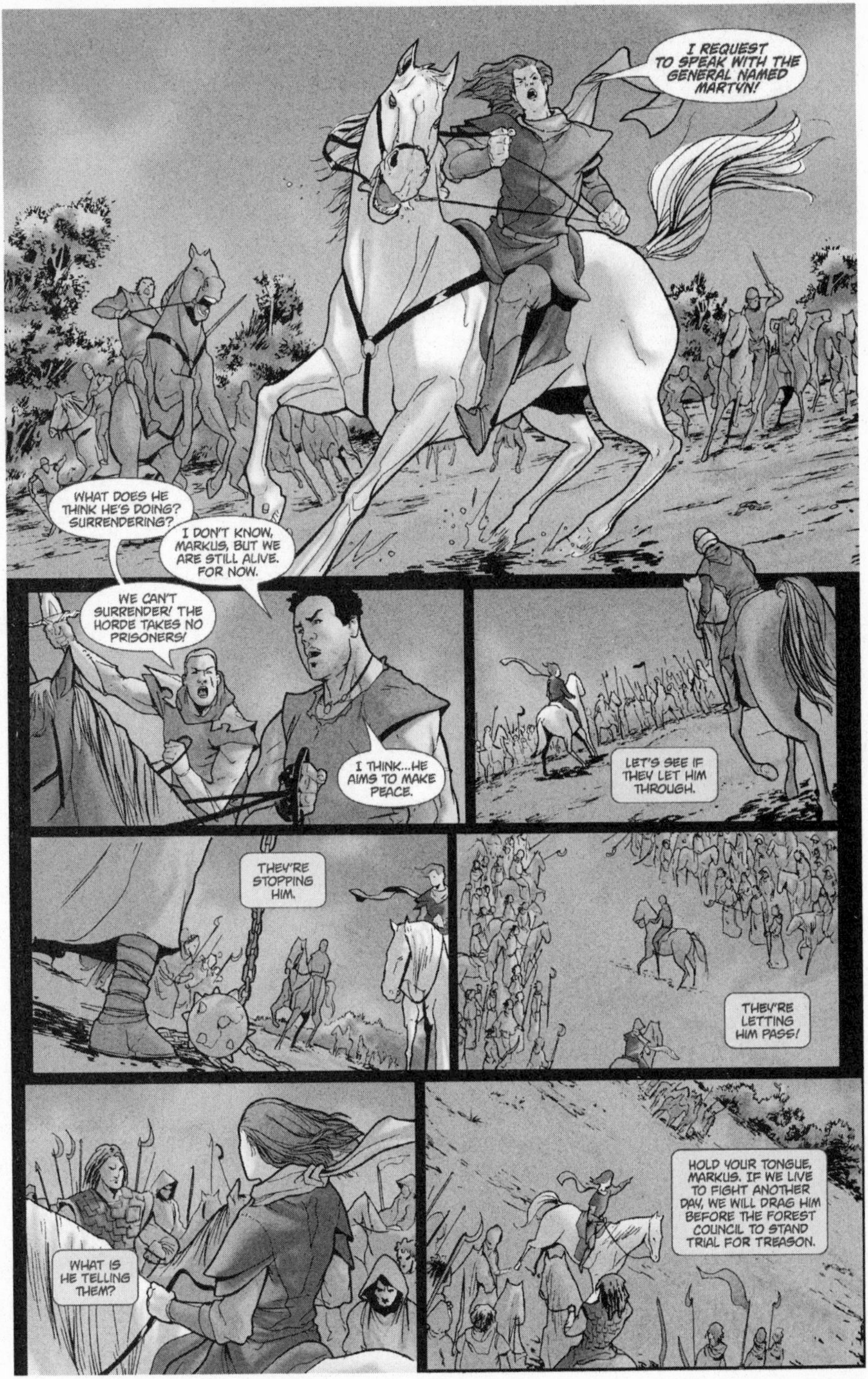

I REQUEST TO SPEAK WITH THE GENERAL NAMED MARTYN!
WHAT DOES HE THINK HE'S DOING? SURRENDERING?
I DON'T KNOW, MARKUS, BUT WE ARE STILL ALIVE. FOR NOW.
WE CAN'T SURRENDER! THE HORDE TAKES NO PRISONERS!
I THINK...HE AIMS TO MAKE PEACE.
LET'S SEE IF THEY LET HIM THROUGH.
THEY'RE STOPPING HIM.
THEY'RE LETTING HIM PASS!
WHAT IS HE TELLING THEM?
HOLD YOUR TONGUE, MARKUS. IF WE LIVE TO FIGHT ANOTHER DAY, WE WILL DRAG HIM BEFORE THE FOREST COUNCIL TO STAND TRIAL FOR TREASON.

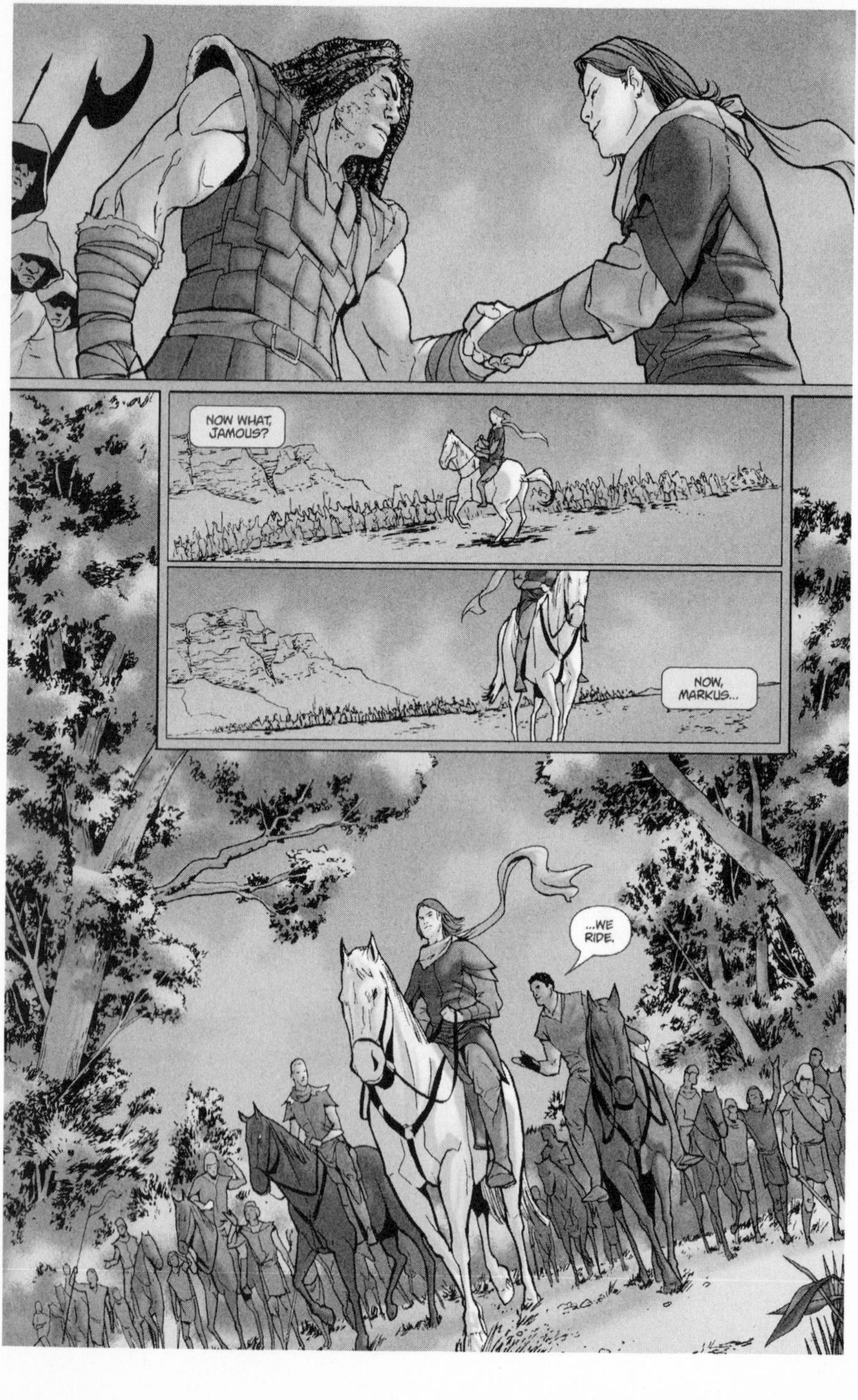
NOW WHAT, JAMOUS?
NOW, MARKUS...
...WE RIDE.

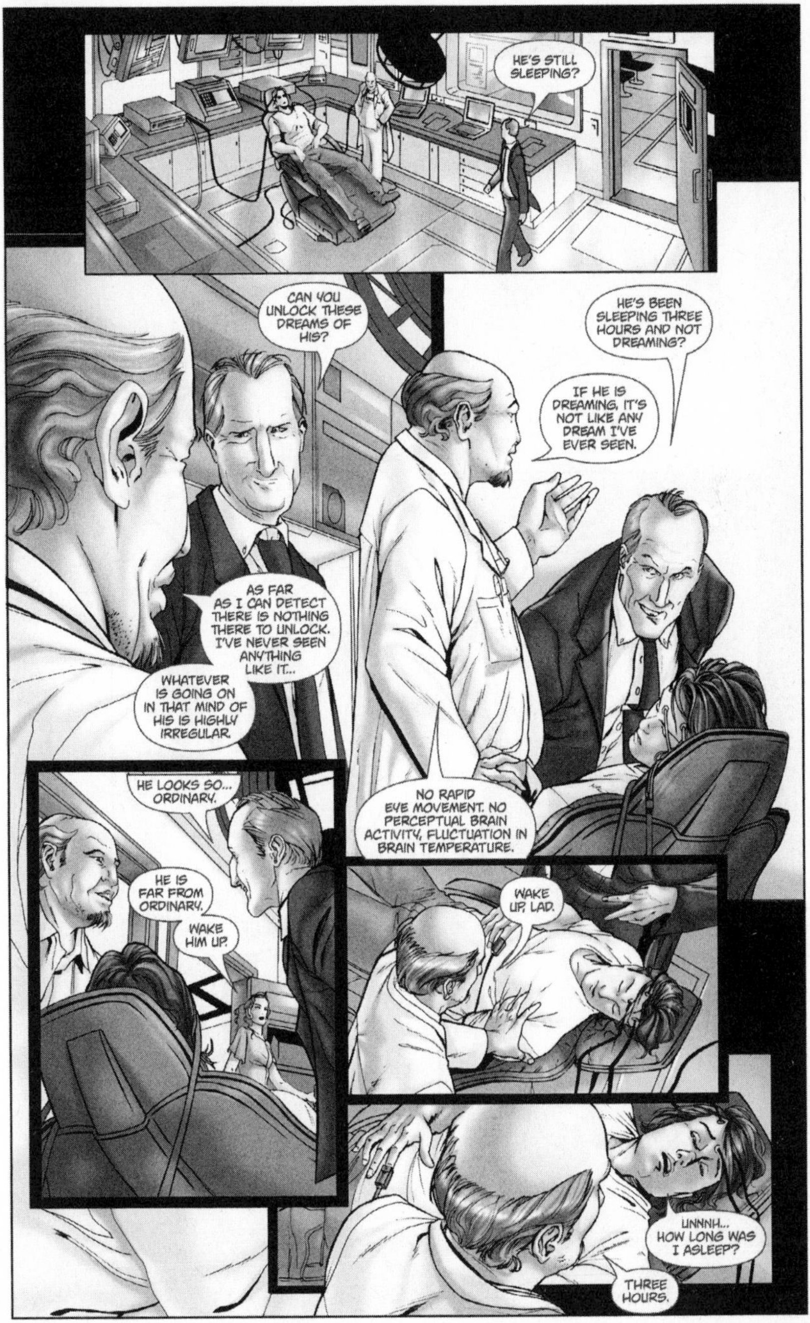

HE'S STILL SLEEPING?
CAN YOU UNLOCK THESE DREAMS OF HIS?
HE'S BEEN SLEEPING THREE HOURS AND NOT DREAMING?
IF HE IS DREAMING, IT'S NOT LIKE ANY DREAM I'VE EVER SEEN.
AS FAR AS I CAN DETECT THERE IS NOTHING THERE TO UNLOCK. I'VE NEVER SEEN ANYTHING LIKE IT...
WHATEVER IS GOING ON IN THAT MIND OF HIS IS HIGHLY IRREGULAR.
NO RAPID EYE MOVEMENT. NO PERCEPTUAL BRAIN ACTIVITY, FLUCTUATION IN BRAIN TEMPERATURE.
HE LOOKS SO... ORDINARY.
HE IS FAR FROM ORDINARY.
WAKE HIM UP.
WAKE UP, LAD.
UNNNH... HOW LONG WAS I ASLEEP?
THREE HOURS.

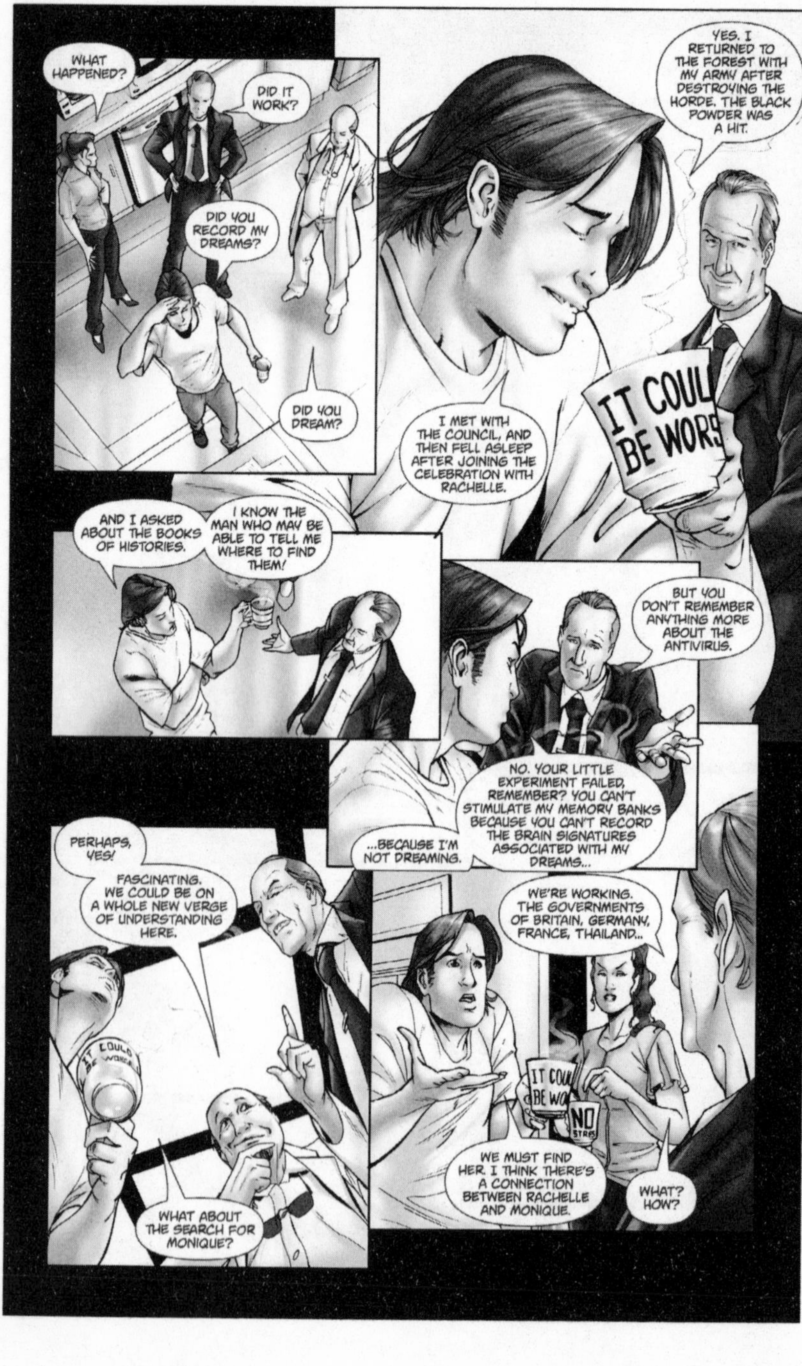

WHAT HAPPENED?
DID IT WORK?
DID YOU RECORD MY DREAMS?
DID YOU DREAM?
YES. I RETURNED TO THE FOREST WITH MY ARMY AFTER DESTROYING THE HORDE. THE BLACK POWDER WAS A HIT.
I MET WITH THE COUNCIL, AND THEN FELL ASLEEP AFTER JOINING THE CELEBRATION WITH RACHELLE.
IT COUL BE WORS
AND I ASKED ABOUT THE BOOKS OF HISTORIES.
I KNOW THE MAN WHO MAY BE ABLE TO TELL ME WHERE TO FIND THEM!
BUT YOU DON'T REMEMBER ANYTHING MORE ABOUT THE ANTIVIRUS.
NO. YOUR LITTLE EXPERIMENT FAILED, REMEMBER? YOU CAN'T STIMULATE MY MEMORY BANKS BECAUSE YOU CAN'T RECORD THE BRAIN SIGNATURES ASSOCIATED WITH MY DREAMS...
...BECAUSE I'M NOT DREAMING.
PERHAPS, YES!
FASCINATING. WE COULD BE ON A WHOLE NEW VERGE OF UNDERSTANDING HERE.
WHAT ABOUT THE SEARCH FOR MONIQUE?
WE'RE WORKING. THE GOVERNMENTS OF BRITAIN, GERMANY, FRANCE, THAILAND...
IT COUL BE WO
NO
WE MUST FIND HER. I THINK THERE'S A CONNECTION BETWEEN RACHELLE AND MONIQUE.
WHAT? HOW?

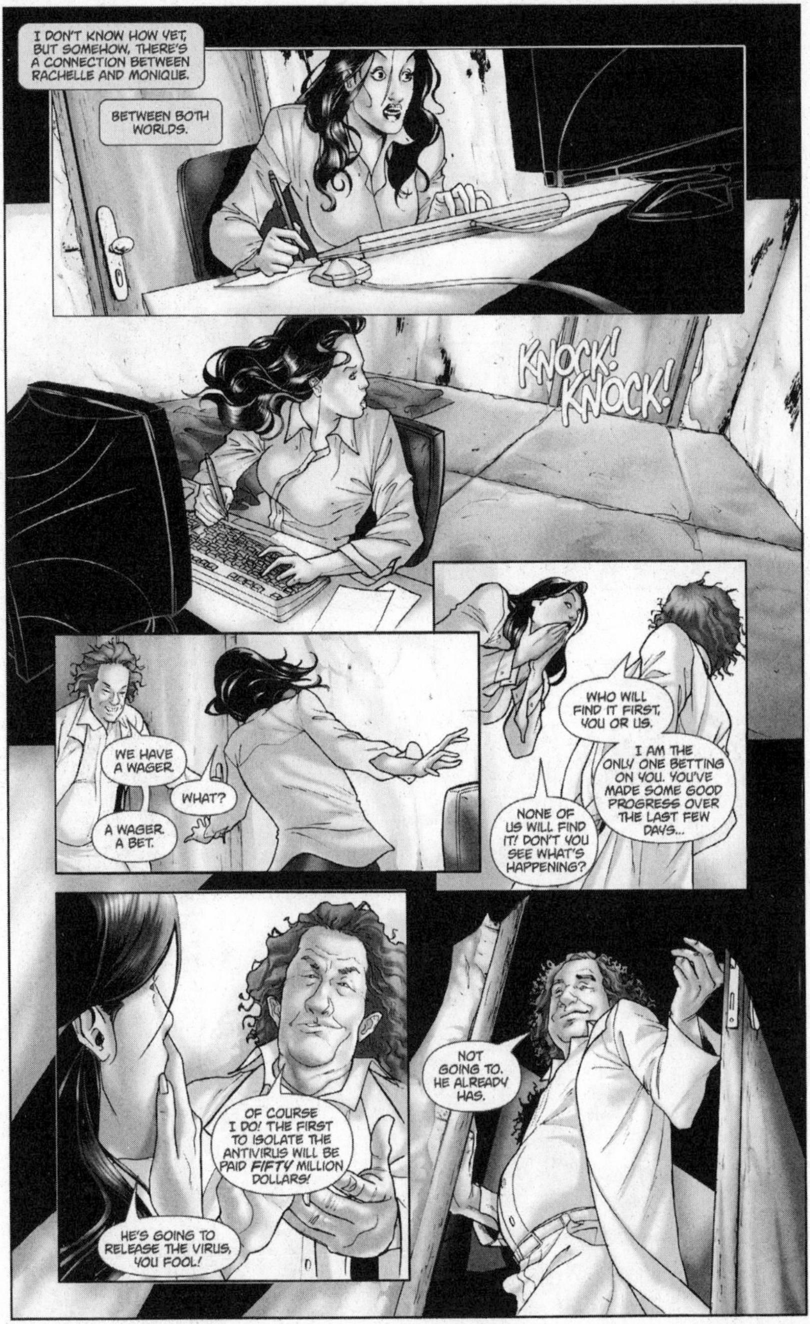
I DON'T KNOW HOW YET, BUT SOMEHOW, THERE'S A CONNECTION BETWEEN RACHELLE AND MONIQUE.
BETWEEN BOTH WORLDS.
KNOCK! KNOCK!
WE HAVE A WAGER.
WHAT?
A WAGER. A BET.
WHO WILL FIND IT FIRST, YOU OR US.
I AM THE ONLY ONE BETTING ON YOU. YOU'VE MADE SOME GOOD PROGRESS OVER THE LAST FEW DAYS...
NONE OF US WILL FIND IT! DON'T YOU SEE WHAT'S HAPPENING?
HE'S GOING TO RELEASE THE VIRUS, YOU FOOL!
OF COURSE I DO! THE FIRST TO ISOLATE THE ANTIVIRUS WILL BE PAID FIFTY MILLION DOLLARS!
NOT GOING TO. HE ALREADY HAS.

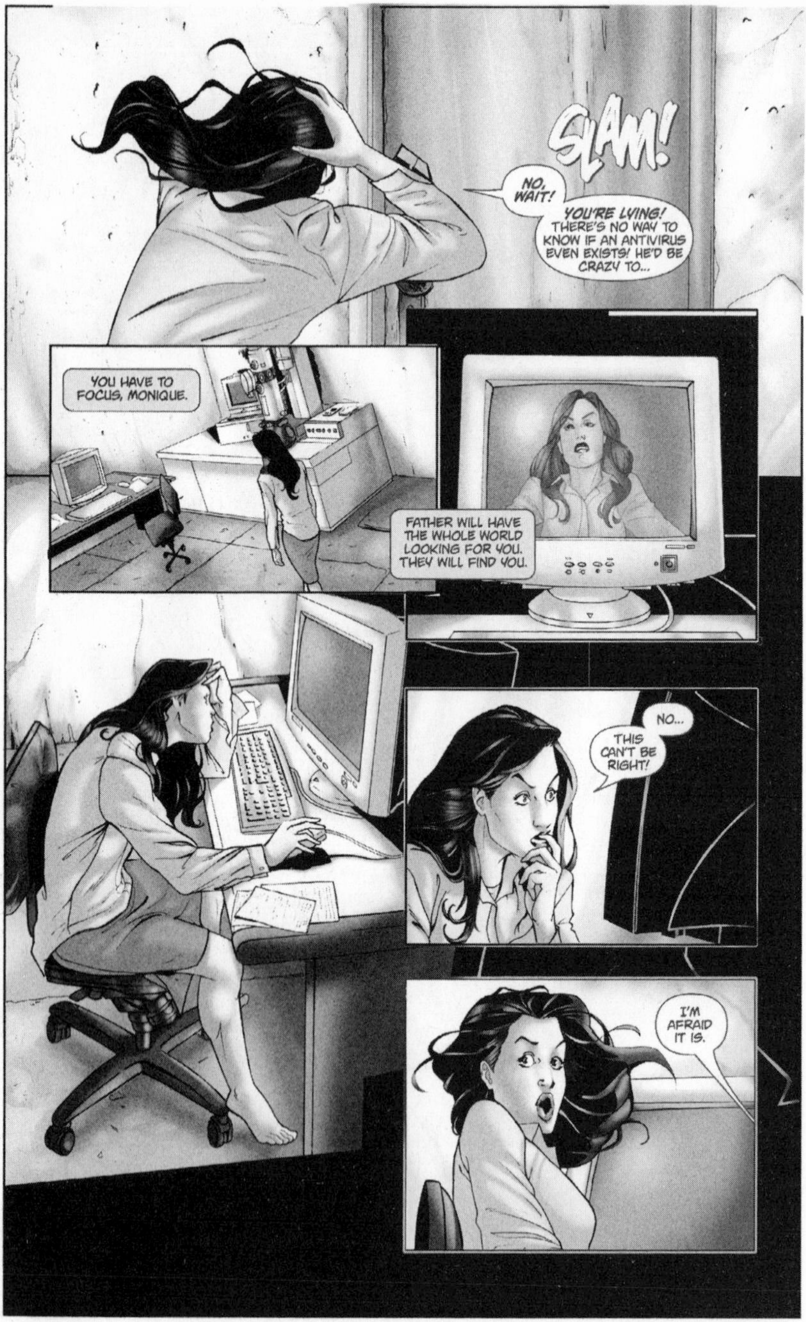
SLAM!
NO, WAIT!
YOU'RE LYING! THERE'S NO WAY TO KNOW IF AN ANTIVIRUS EVEN EXISTS! HE'D BE CRAZY TO...
YOU HAVE TO FOCUS, MONIQUE.
FATHER WILL HAVE THE WHOLE WORLD LOOKING FOR YOU. THEY WILL FIND YOU.
NO...
THIS CAN'T BE RIGHT!
I'M AFRAID IT IS.

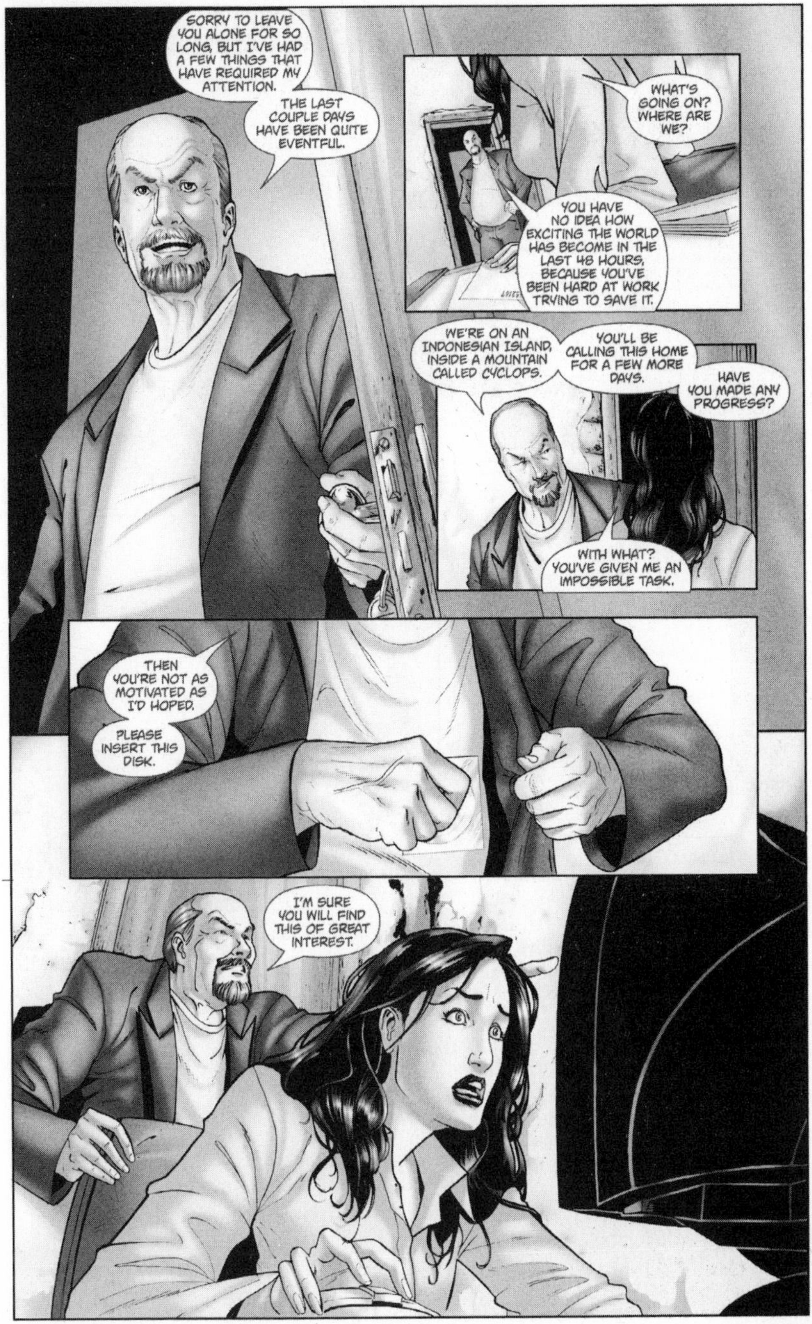

SORRY TO LEAVE YOU ALONE FOR SO LONG, BUT I'VE HAD A FEW THINGS THAT HAVE REQUIRED MY ATTENTION.
THE LAST COUPLE DAYS HAVE BEEN QUITE EVENTFUL.
WHAT'S GOING ON? WHERE ARE WE?
YOU HAVE NO IDEA HOW EXCITING THE WORLD HAS BECOME IN THE LAST 48 HOURS, BECAUSE YOU'VE BEEN HARD AT WORK TRYING TO SAVE IT.
WE'RE ON AN INDONESIAN ISLAND, INSIDE A MOUNTAIN CALLED CYCLOPS.
YOU'LL BE CALLING THIS HOME FOR A FEW MORE DAYS.
HAVE YOU MADE ANY PROGRESS?
WITH WHAT? YOU'VE GIVEN ME AN IMPOSSIBLE TASK.
THEN YOU'RE NOT AS MOTIVATED AS I'D HOPED.
PLEASE INSERT THIS DISK.
I'M SURE YOU WILL FIND THIS OF GREAT INTEREST.

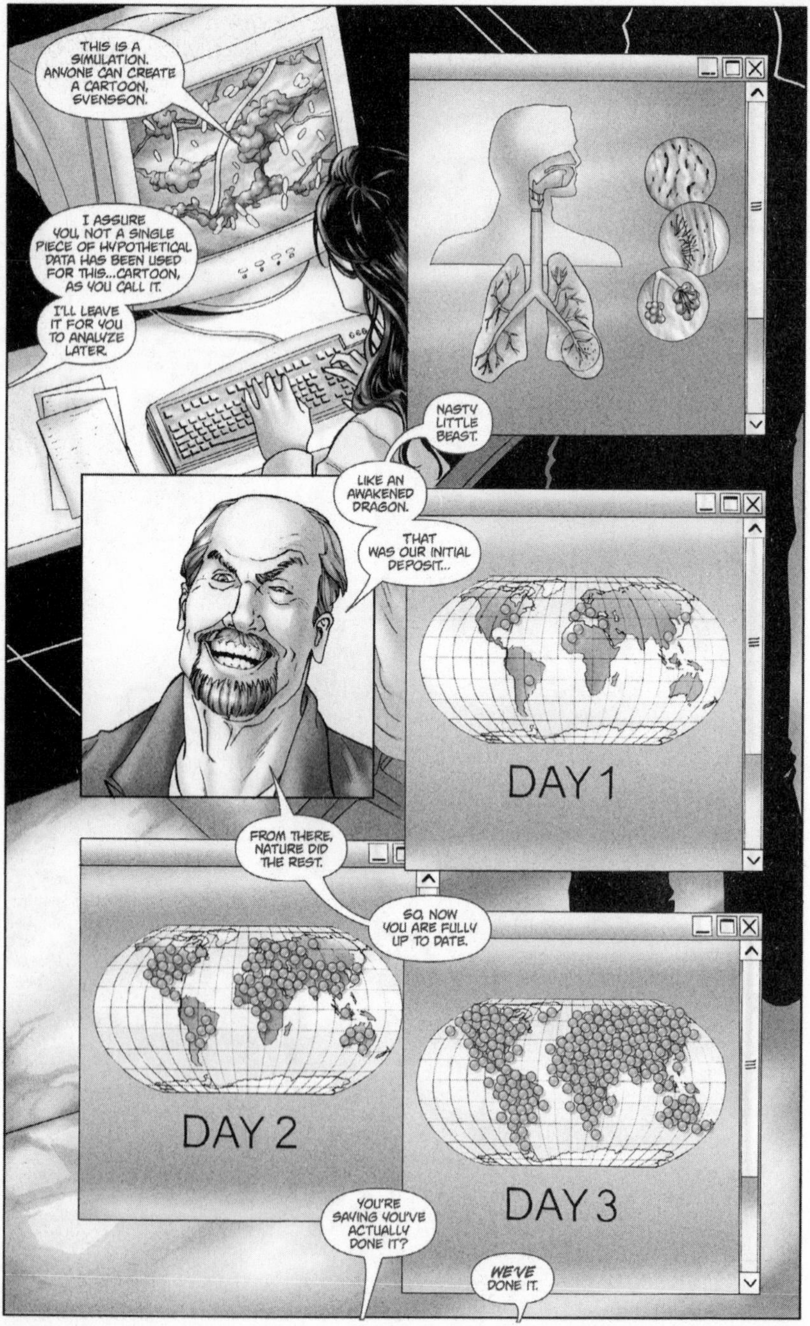
THIS IS A SIMULATION. ANYONE CAN CREATE A CARTOON, SVENSSON.
I ASSURE YOU, NOT A SINGLE PIECE OF HYPOTHETICAL DATA HAS BEEN USED FOR THIS...CARTOON, AS YOU CALL IT.
I'LL LEAVE IT FOR YOU TO ANALYZE LATER.
NASTY LITTLE BEAST.
LIKE AN AWAKENED DRAGON.
THAT WAS OUR INITIAL DEPOSIT...
DAY 1
FROM THERE, NATURE DID THE REST.
SO, NOW YOU ARE FULLY UP TO DATE.
DAY 2
DAY 3
YOU'RE SAYING YOU'VE ACTUALLY DONE IT?
WE'VE DONE IT.

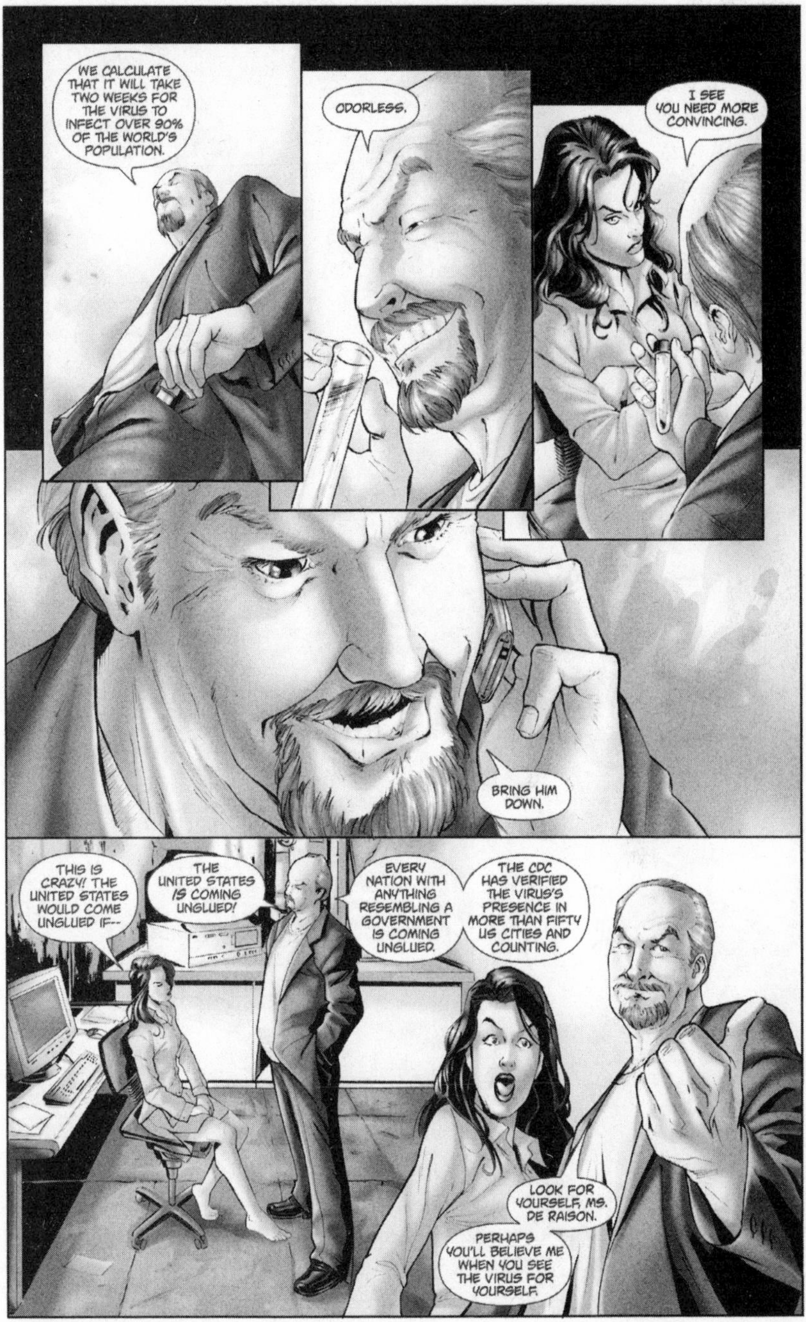
WE CALCULATE THAT IT WILL TAKE TWO WEEKS FOR THE VIRUS TO INFECT OVER 90% OF THE WORLD'S POPULATION.
ODORLESS.
I SEE YOU NEED MORE CONVINCING.
BRING HIM DOWN.
THIS IS CRAZY! THE UNITED STATES WOULD COME UNGLUED IF--
THE UNITED STATES IS COMING UNGLUED!
EVERY NATION WITH ANYTHING RESEMBLING A GOVERNMENT IS COMING UNGLUED.
THE CDC HAS VERIFIED THE VIRUS'S PRESENCE IN MORE THAN FIFTY US CITIES AND COUNTING.
LOOK FOR YOURSELF, MS. DE RAISON.
PERHAPS YOU'LL BELIEVE ME WHEN YOU SEE THE VIRUS FOR YOURSELF.

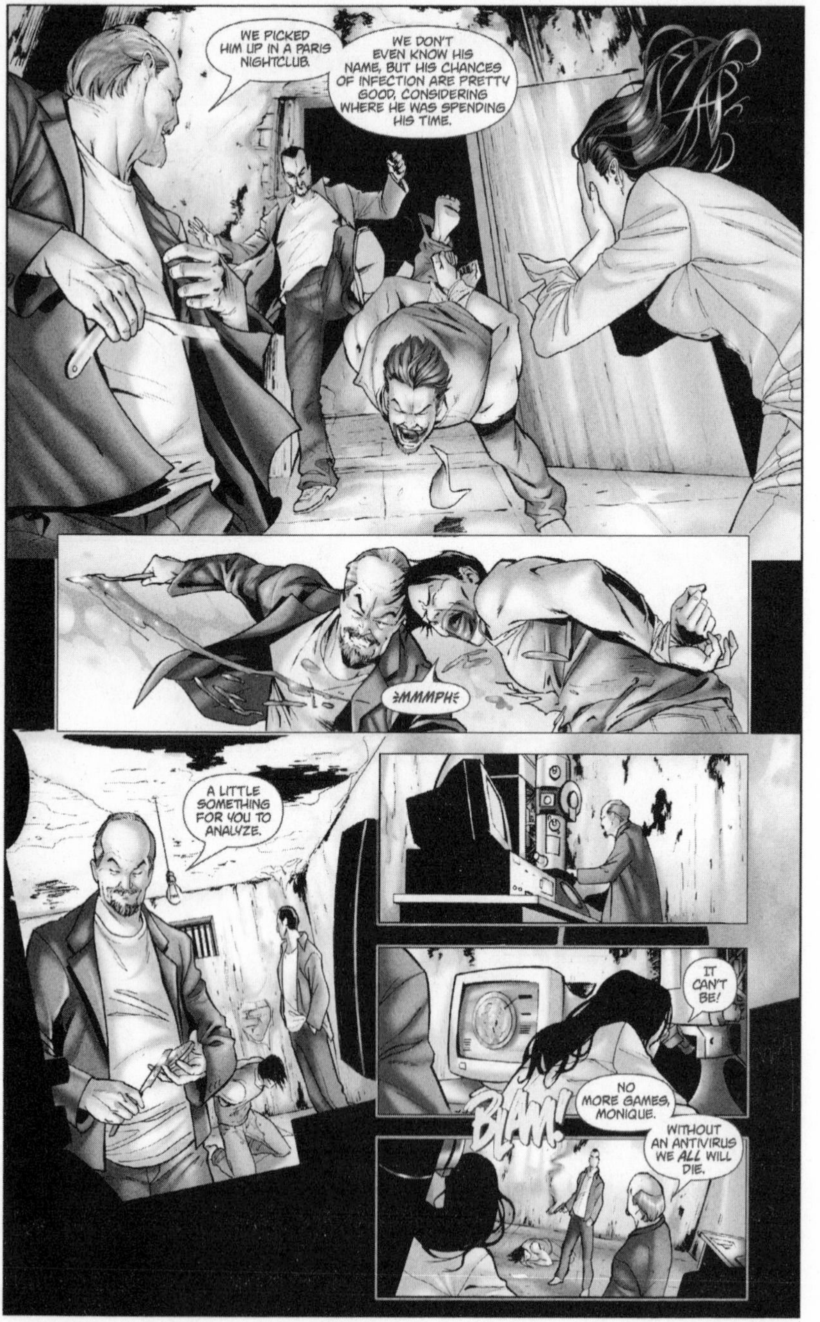
WE PICKED HIM UP IN A PARIS NIGHTCLUB.
WE DON'T EVEN KNOW HIS NAME, BUT HIS CHANCES OF INFECTION ARE PRETTY GOOD, CONSIDERING WHERE HE WAS SPENDING HIS TIME.
MMMPH
A LITTLE SOMETHING FOR YOU TO ANALYZE.
IT CAN'T BE!
BLAM!
NO MORE GAMES, MONIQUE.
WITHOUT AN ANTIVIRUS WE ALL WILL DIE.

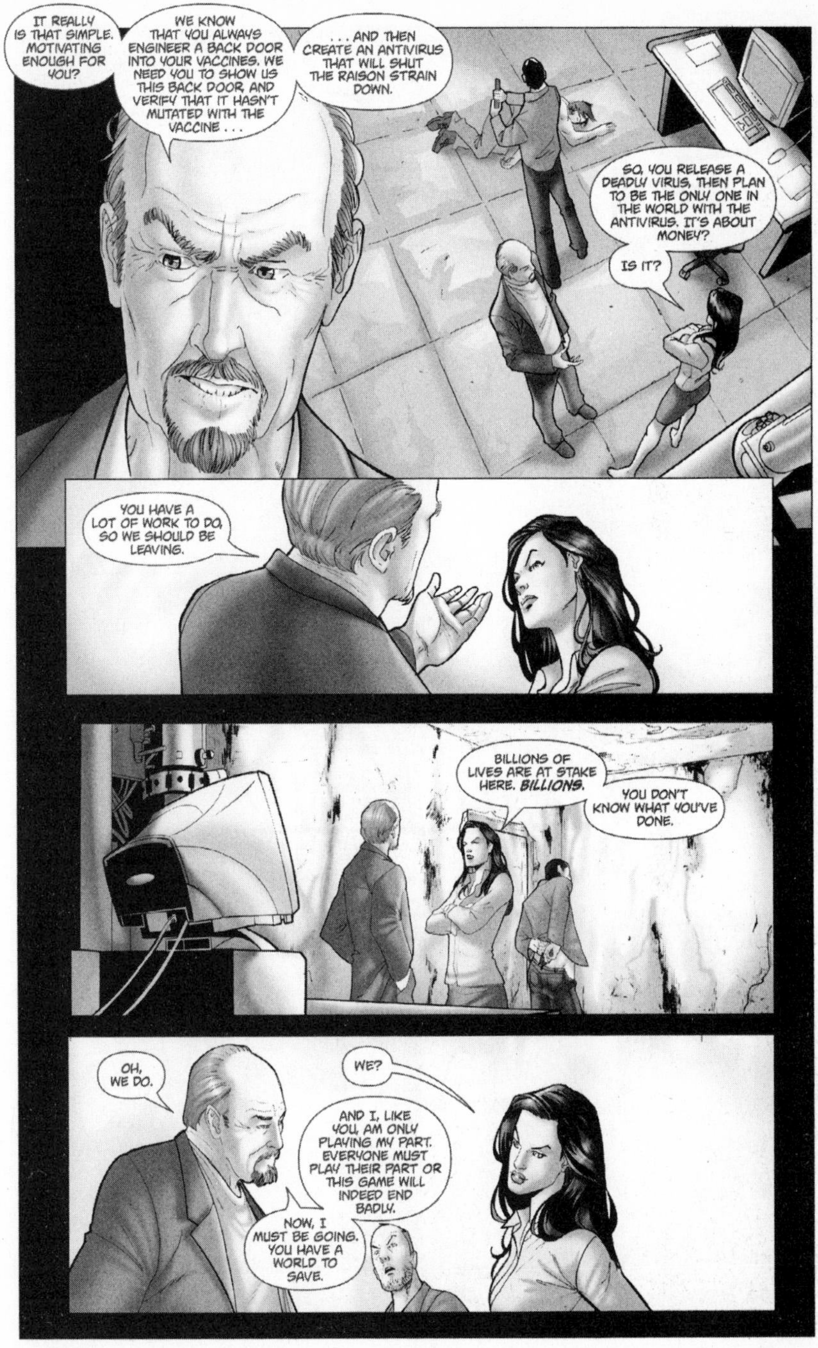
IT REALLY IS THAT SIMPLE. MOTIVATING ENOUGH FOR YOU?
WE KNOW THAT YOU ALWAYS ENGINEER A BACK DOOR INTO YOUR VACCINES. WE NEED YOU TO SHOW US THIS BACK DOOR AND VERIFY THAT IT HASN'T MUTATED WITH THE VACCINE . . .
. . . AND THEN CREATE AN ANTIVIRUS THAT WILL SHUT THE RAISON STRAIN DOWN.
SO, YOU RELEASE A DEADLY VIRUS, THEN PLAN TO BE THE ONLY ONE IN THE WORLD WITH THE ANTIVIRUS. IT'S ABOUT MONEY?
IS IT?
YOU HAVE A LOT OF WORK TO DO, SO WE SHOULD BE LEAVING.
BILLIONS OF LIVES ARE AT STAKE HERE. BILLIONS.
YOU DON'T KNOW WHAT YOU'VE DONE.
OH, WE DO.
WE?
AND I, LIKE YOU, AM ONLY PLAYING MY PART. EVERYONE MUST PLAY THEIR PART OR THIS GAME WILL INDEED END BADLY.
NOW, I MUST BE GOING. YOU HAVE A WORLD TO SAVE.

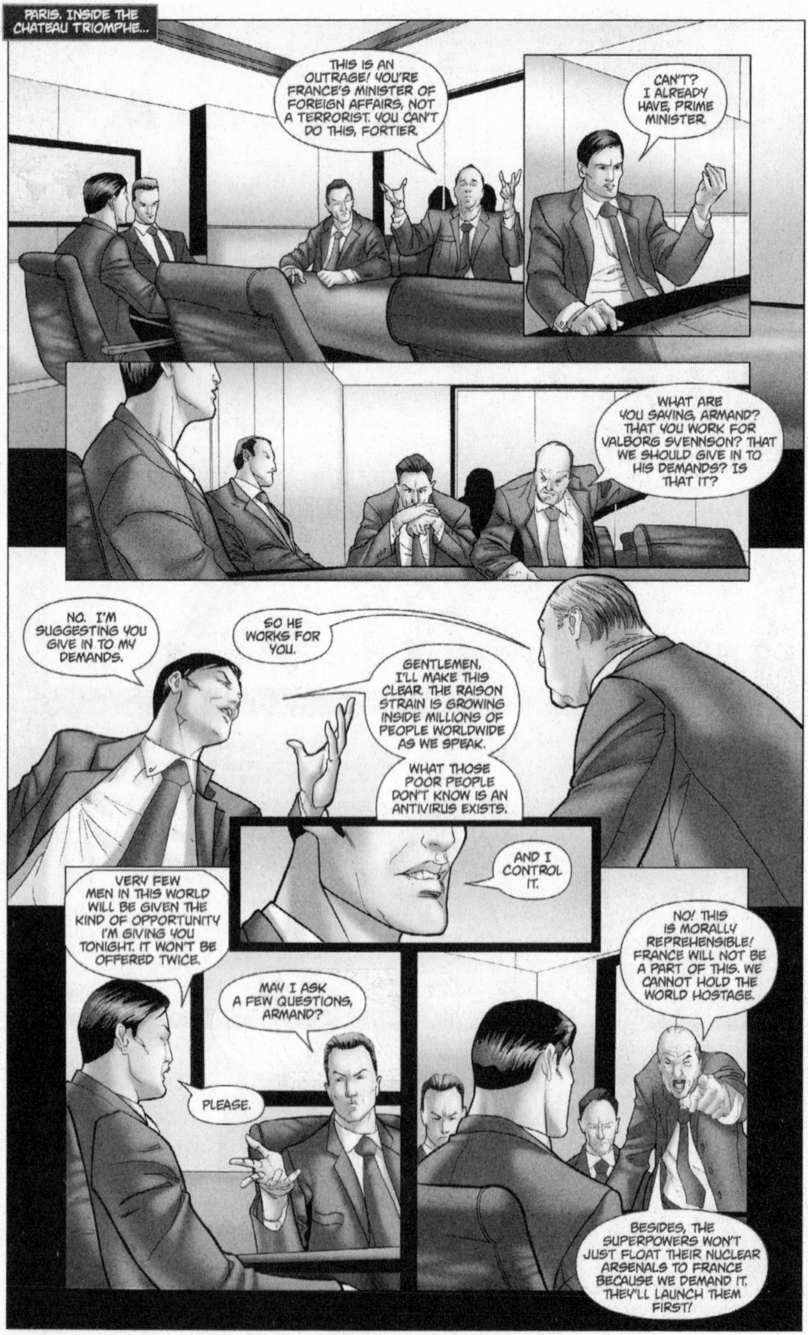
PARIS. INSIDE THE CHATEAU TRIOMPHE...
THIS IS AN OUTRAGE! YOU'RE FRANCE'S MINISTER OF FOREIGN AFFAIRS, NOT A TERRORIST. YOU CAN'T DO THIS, FORTIER.
CAN'T? I ALREADY HAVE, PRIME MINISTER.
WHAT ARE YOU SAYING, ARMAND? THAT YOU WORK FOR VALBORG SVENNSON? THAT WE SHOULD GIVE IN TO HIS DEMANDS? IS THAT IT?
NO. I'M SUGGESTING YOU GIVE IN TO MY DEMANDS.
SO HE WORKS FOR YOU.
GENTLEMEN, I'LL MAKE THIS CLEAR. THE RAISON STRAIN IS GROWING INSIDE MILLIONS OF PEOPLE WORLDWIDE AS WE SPEAK.
WHAT THOSE POOR PEOPLE DON'T KNOW IS AN ANTIVIRUS EXISTS.
AND I CONTROL IT.
VERY FEW MEN IN THIS WORLD WILL BE GIVEN THE KIND OF OPPORTUNITY I'M GIVING YOU TONIGHT. IT WON'T BE OFFERED TWICE.
MAY I ASK A FEW QUESTIONS, ARMAND?
PLEASE.
NO! THIS IS MORALLY REPREHENSIBLE! FRANCE WILL NOT BE A PART OF THIS. WE CANNOT HOLD THE WORLD HOSTAGE.
BESIDES, THE SUPERPOWERS WON'T JUST FLOAT THEIR NUCLEAR ARSENALS TO FRANCE BECAUSE WE DEMAND IT. THEY'LL LAUNCH THEM FIRST!

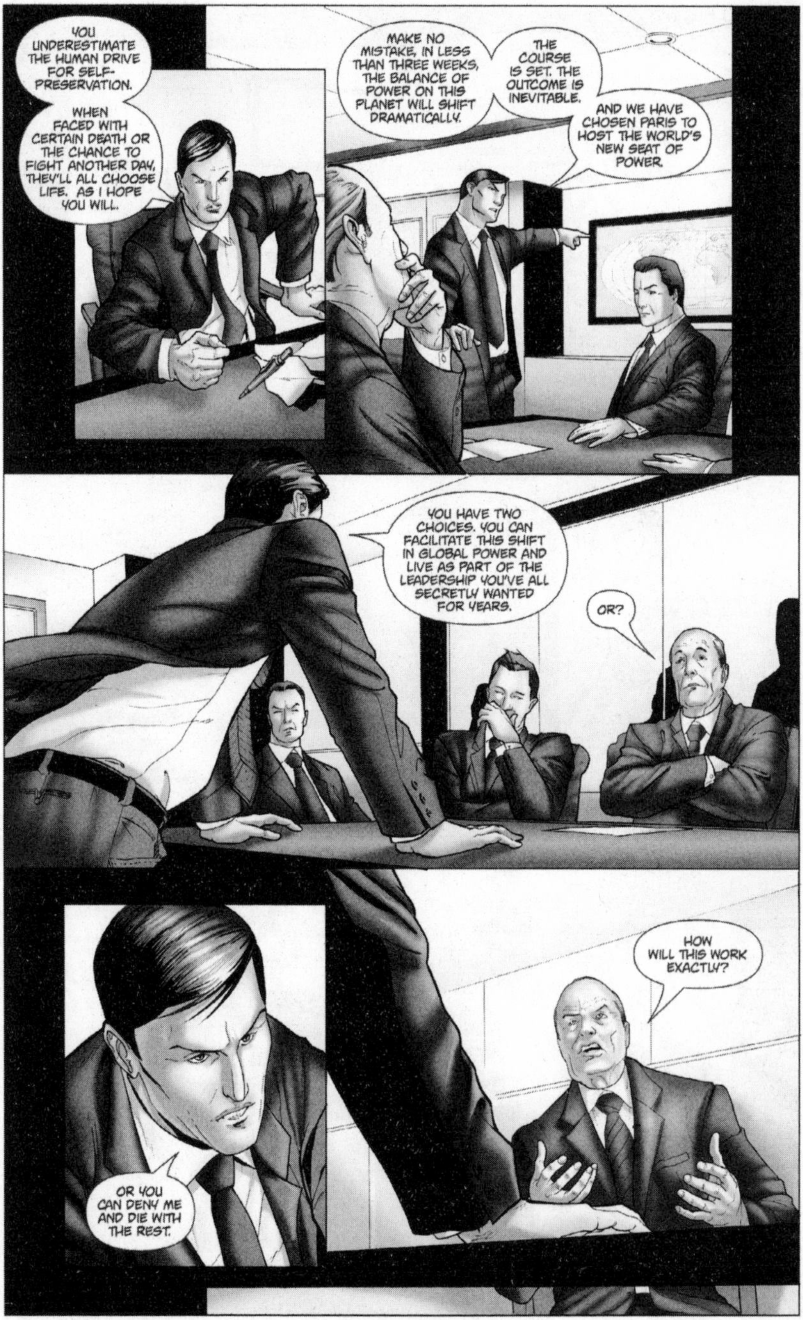
YOU UNDERESTIMATE THE HUMAN DRIVE FOR SELF-PRESERVATION.
WHEN FACED WITH CERTAIN DEATH OR THE CHANCE TO FIGHT ANOTHER DAY, THEY'LL ALL CHOOSE LIFE. AS I HOPE YOU WILL.
MAKE NO MISTAKE, IN LESS THAN THREE WEEKS, THE BALANCE OF POWER ON THIS PLANET WILL SHIFT DRAMATICALLY.
THE COURSE IS SET. THE OUTCOME IS INEVITABLE.
AND WE HAVE CHOSEN PARIS TO HOST THE WORLD'S NEW SEAT OF POWER.
YOU HAVE TWO CHOICES. YOU CAN FACILITATE THIS SHIFT IN GLOBAL POWER AND LIVE AS PART OF THE LEADERSHIP YOU'VE ALL SECRETLY WANTED FOR YEARS.
OR?
OR YOU CAN DENY ME AND DIE WITH THE REST.
HOW WILL THIS WORK EXACTLY?

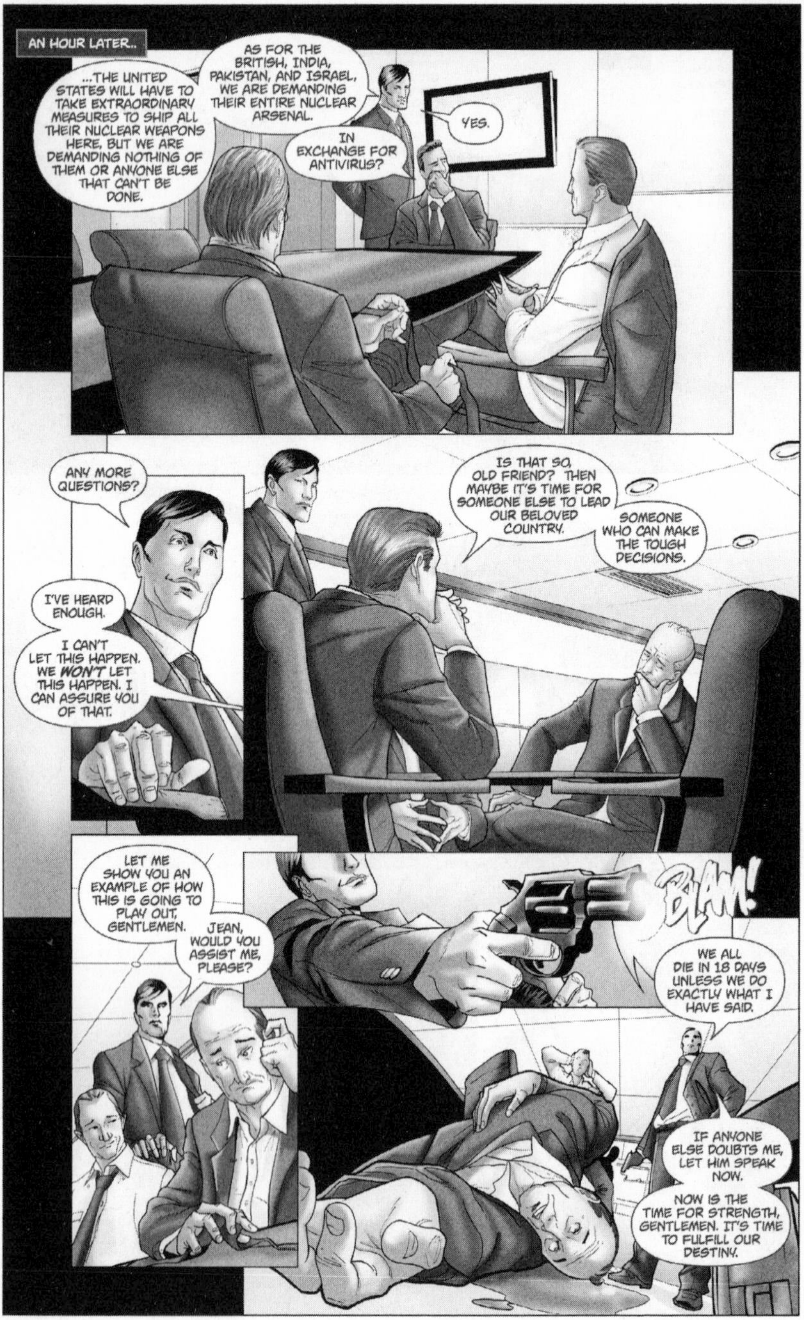
AN HOUR LATER..
...THE UNITED STATES WILL HAVE TO TAKE EXTRAORDINARY MEASURES TO SHIP ALL THEIR NUCLEAR WEAPONS HERE, BUT WE ARE DEMANDING NOTHING OF THEM OR ANYONE ELSE THAT CAN'T BE DONE.
AS FOR THE BRITISH, INDIA, PAKISTAN, AND ISRAEL, WE ARE DEMANDING THEIR ENTIRE NUCLEAR ARSENAL.
IN EXCHANGE FOR ANTIVIRUS?
YES.
ANY MORE QUESTIONS?
IS THAT SO, OLD FRIEND? THEN MAYBE IT'S TIME FOR SOMEONE ELSE TO LEAD OUR BELOVED COUNTRY.
SOMEONE WHO CAN MAKE THE TOUGH DECISIONS.
I'VE HEARD ENOUGH.
I CAN'T LET THIS HAPPEN. WE WON'T LET THIS HAPPEN. I CAN ASSURE YOU OF THAT.
LET ME SHOW YOU AN EXAMPLE OF HOW THIS IS GOING TO PLAY OUT, GENTLEMEN.
JEAN, WOULD YOU ASSIST ME, PLEASE?
BLAM!
WE ALL DIE IN 18 DAYS UNLESS WE DO EXACTLY WHAT I HAVE SAID.
IF ANYONE ELSE DOUBTS ME, LET HIM SPEAK NOW.
NOW IS THE TIME FOR STRENGTH, GENTLEMEN. IT'S TIME TO FULFILL OUR DESTINY.

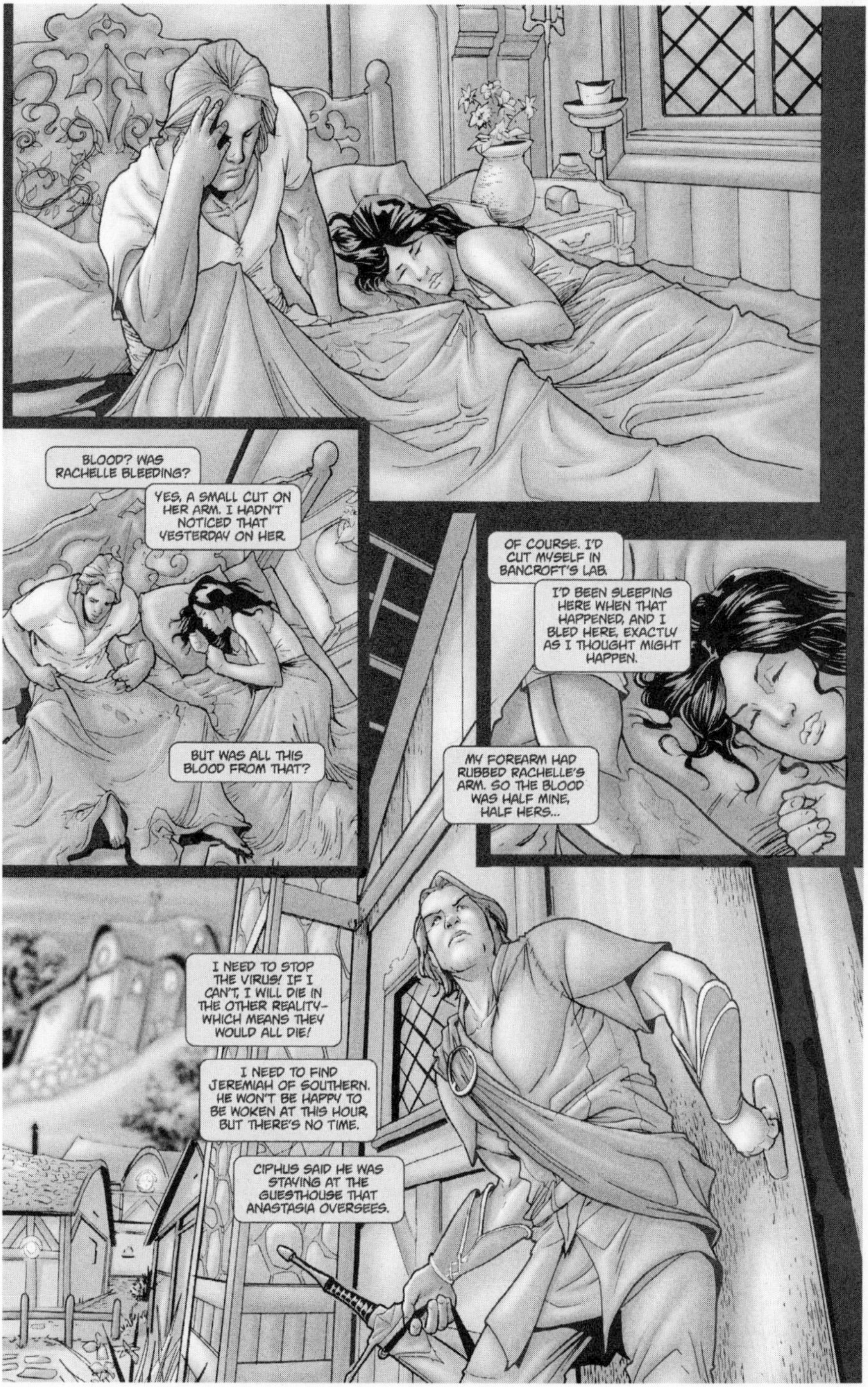
BLOOD? WAS RACHELLE BLEEDING?
YES, A SMALL CUT ON HER ARM. I HADN'T NOTICED THAT YESTERDAY ON HER.
BUT WAS ALL THIS BLOOD FROM THAT?
OF COURSE. I'D CUT MYSELF IN BANCROFT'S LAB.
I'D BEEN SLEEPING HERE WHEN THAT HAPPENED, AND I BLED HERE, EXACTLY AS I THOUGHT MIGHT HAPPEN.
MY FOREARM HAD RUBBED RACHELLE'S ARM. SO THE BLOOD WAS HALF MINE, HALF HERS...
I NEED TO STOP THE VIRUS! IF I CAN'T, I WILL DIE IN THE OTHER REALITY-WHICH MEANS THEY WOULD ALL DIE!
I NEED TO FIND JEREMIAH OF SOUTHERN. HE WON'T BE HAPPY TO BE WOKEN AT THIS HOUR, BUT THERE'S NO TIME.
CIPHUS SAID HE WAS STAYING AT THE GUESTHOUSE THAT ANASTASIA OVERSEES.

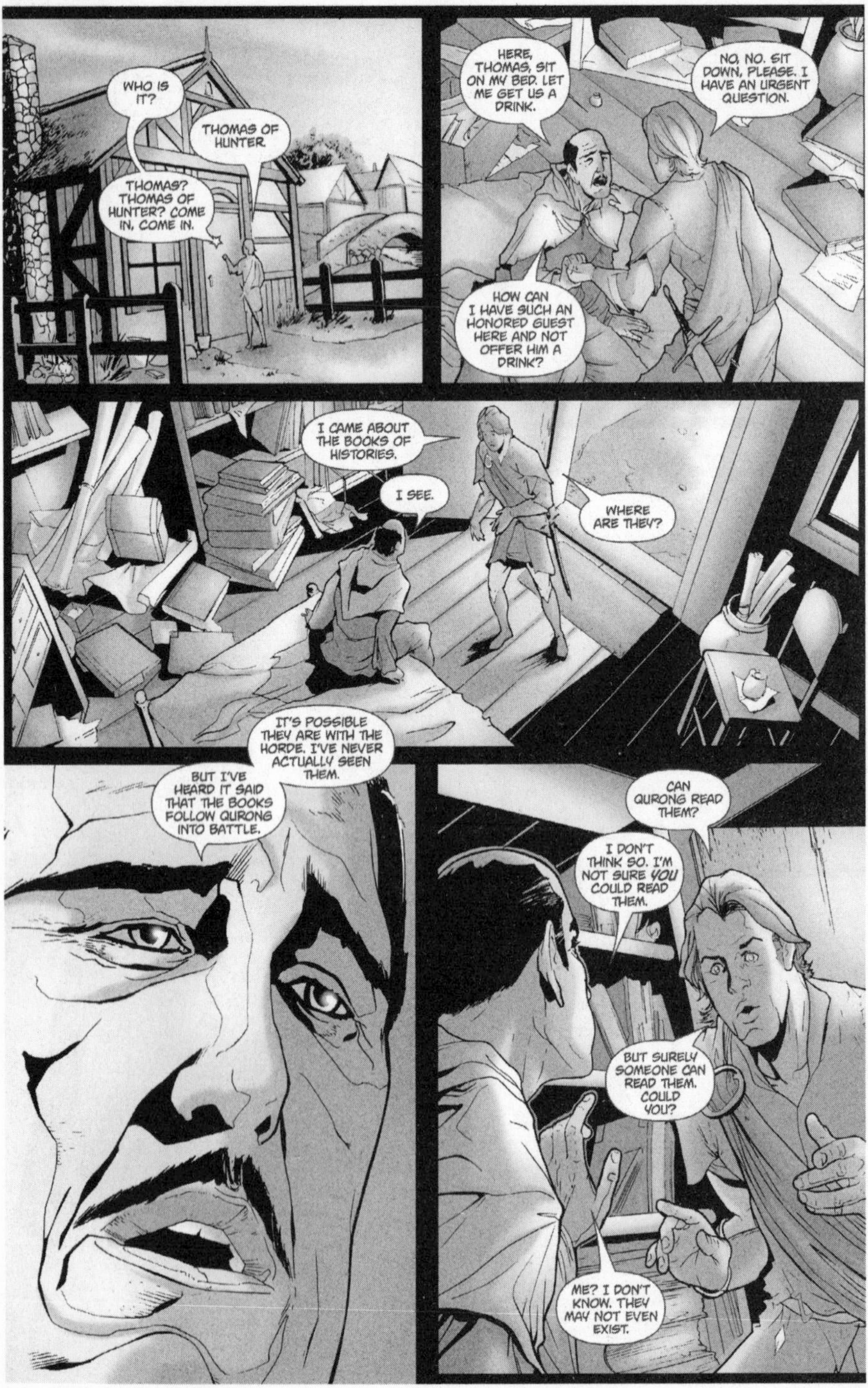
WHO IS IT?
THOMAS OF HUNTER.
THOMAS? THOMAS OF HUNTER? COME IN, COME IN.
HERE, THOMAS, SIT ON MY BED. LET ME GET US A DRINK.
NO, NO. SIT DOWN, PLEASE. I HAVE AN URGENT QUESTION.
HOW CAN I HAVE SUCH AN HONORED GUEST HERE AND NOT OFFER HIM A DRINK?
I CAME ABOUT THE BOOKS OF HISTORIES.
I SEE.
WHERE ARE THEY?
IT'S POSSIBLE THEY ARE WITH THE HORDE. I'VE NEVER ACTUALLY SEEN THEM.
BUT I'VE HEARD IT SAID THAT THE BOOKS FOLLOW QURONG INTO BATTLE.
CAN QURONG READ THEM?
I DON'T THINK SO. I'M NOT SURE YOU COULD READ THEM.
BUT SURELY SOMEONE CAN READ THEM. COULD YOU?
ME? I DON'T KNOW. THEY MAY NOT EVEN EXIST.

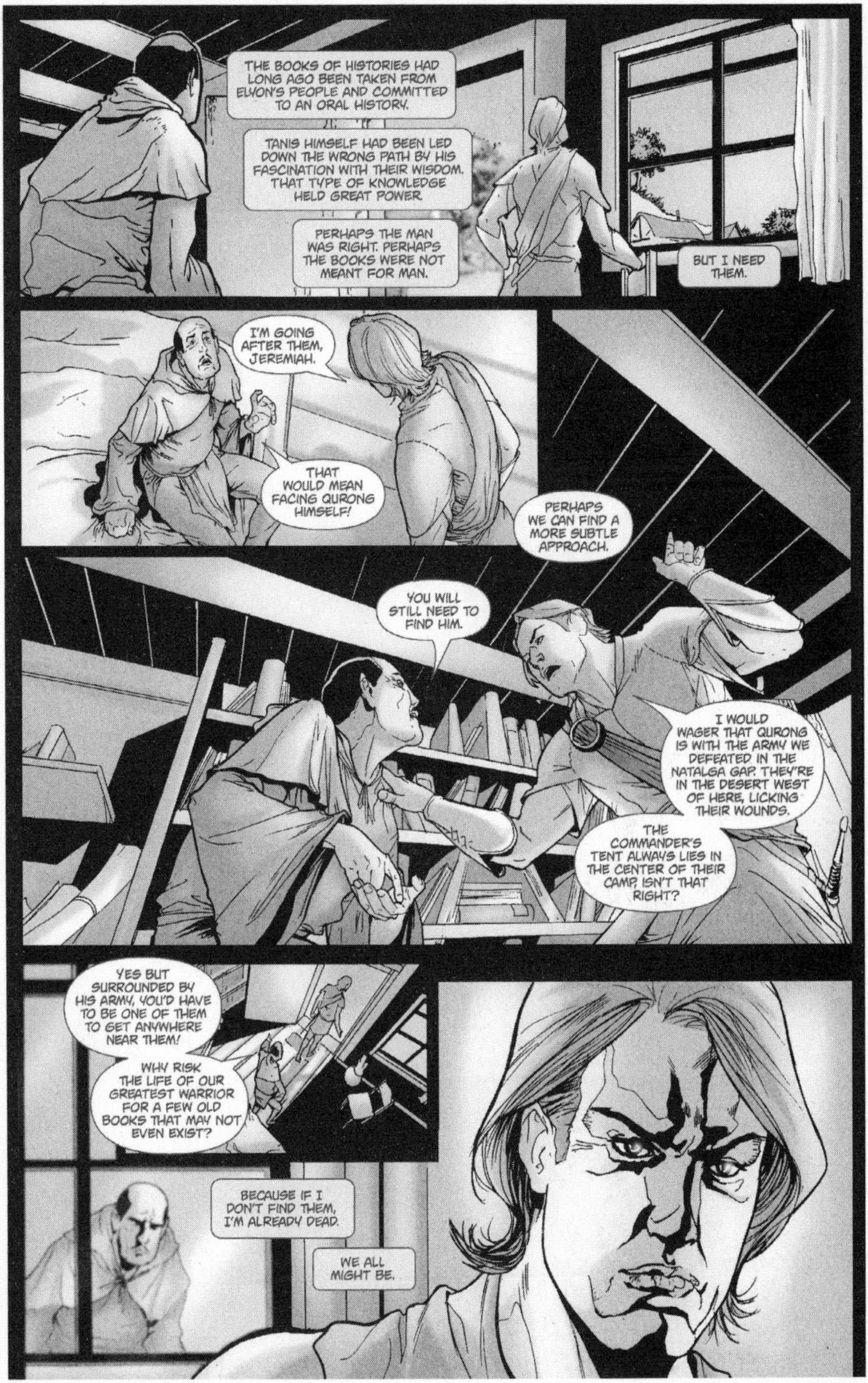
THE BOOKS OF HISTORIES HAD LONG AGO BEEN TAKEN FROM ELYON'S PEOPLE AND COMMITTED TO AN ORAL HISTORY.
TANIS HIMSELF HAD BEEN LED DOWN THE WRONG PATH BY HIS FASCINATION WITH THEIR WISDOM. THAT TYPE OF KNOWLEDGE HELD GREAT POWER.
PERHAPS THE MAN WAS RIGHT. PERHAPS THE BOOKS WERE NOT MEANT FOR MAN.
BUT I NEED THEM.
I'M GOING AFTER THEM, JEREMIAH.
THAT WOULD MEAN FACING QURONG HIMSELF!
PERHAPS WE CAN FIND A MORE SUBTLE APPROACH.
YOU WILL STILL NEED TO FIND HIM.
I WOULD WAGER THAT QURONG IS WITH THE ARMY WE DEFEATED IN THE NATALGA GAP. THEY'RE IN THE DESERT WEST OF HERE, LICKING THEIR WOUNDS.
THE COMMANDER'S TENT ALWAYS LIES IN THE CENTER OF THEIR CAMP, ISN'T THAT RIGHT?
YES BUT SURROUNDED BY HIS ARMY, YOU'D HAVE TO BE ONE OF THEM TO GET ANYWHERE NEAR THEM!
WHY RISK THE LIFE OF OUR GREATEST WARRIOR FOR A FEW OLD BOOKS THAT MAY NOT EVEN EXIST?
BECAUSE IF I DON'T FIND THEM, I'M ALREADY DEAD.
WE ALL MIGHT BE.

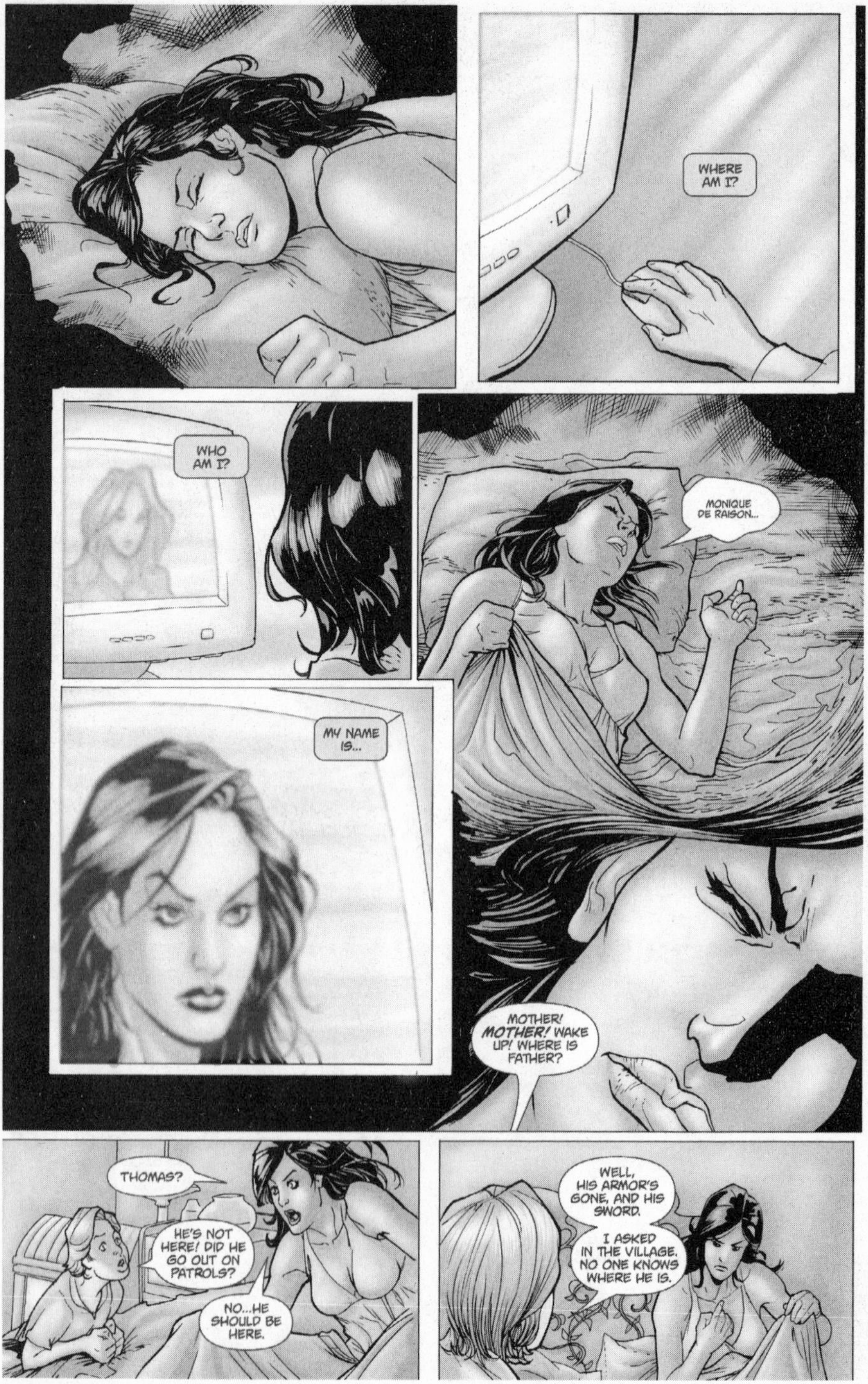
WHERE AM I?
WHO AM I?
MONIQUE DE RAISON...
MY NAME IS...
MOTHER! *MOTHER!* WAKE UP! WHERE IS FATHER?
THOMAS?
HE'S NOT HERE! DID HE GO OUT ON PATROLS?
NO...HE SHOULD BE HERE.
WELL, HIS ARMOR'S GONE, AND HIS SWORD.
I ASKED IN THE VILLAGE. NO ONE KNOWS WHERE HE IS.

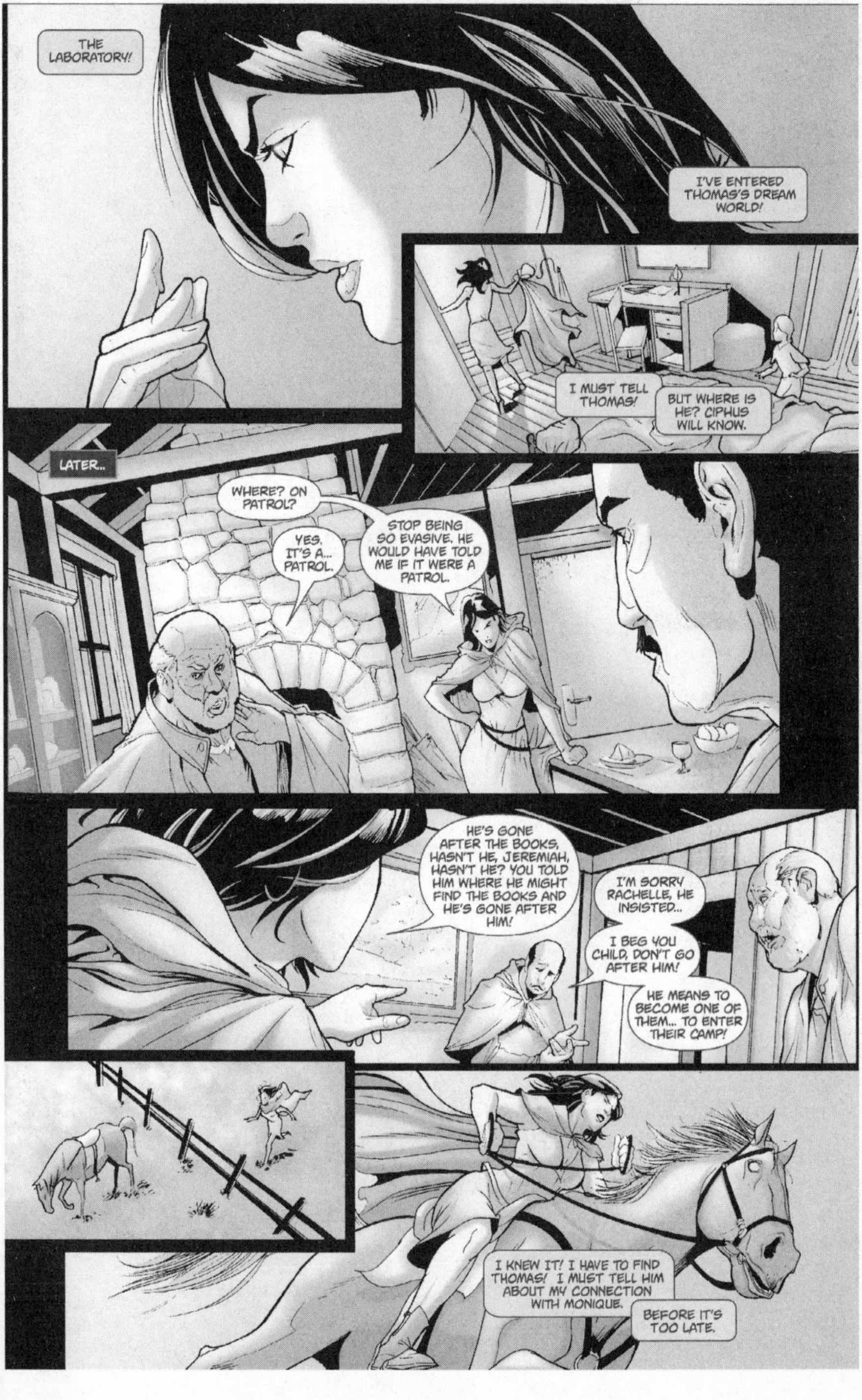
THE LABORATORY!
I'VE ENTERED THOMAS'S DREAM WORLD!
I MUST TELL THOMAS!
BUT WHERE IS HE? CIPHUS WILL KNOW.
LATER...
WHERE? ON PATROL?
YES. IT'S A... PATROL.
STOP BEING SO EVASIVE. HE WOULD HAVE TOLD ME IF IT WERE A PATROL.
HE'S GONE AFTER THE BOOKS, HASN'T HE, JEREMIAH, HASN'T HE? YOU TOLD HIM WHERE HE MIGHT FIND THE BOOKS AND HE'S GONE AFTER HIM!
I'M SORRY RACHELLE, HE INSISTED...
I BEG YOU CHILD, DON'T GO AFTER HIM!
HE MEANS TO BECOME ONE OF THEM... TO ENTER THEIR CAMP!
I KNEW IT! I HAVE TO FIND THOMAS! I MUST TELL HIM ABOUT MY CONNECTION WITH MONIQUE.
BEFORE IT'S TOO LATE.

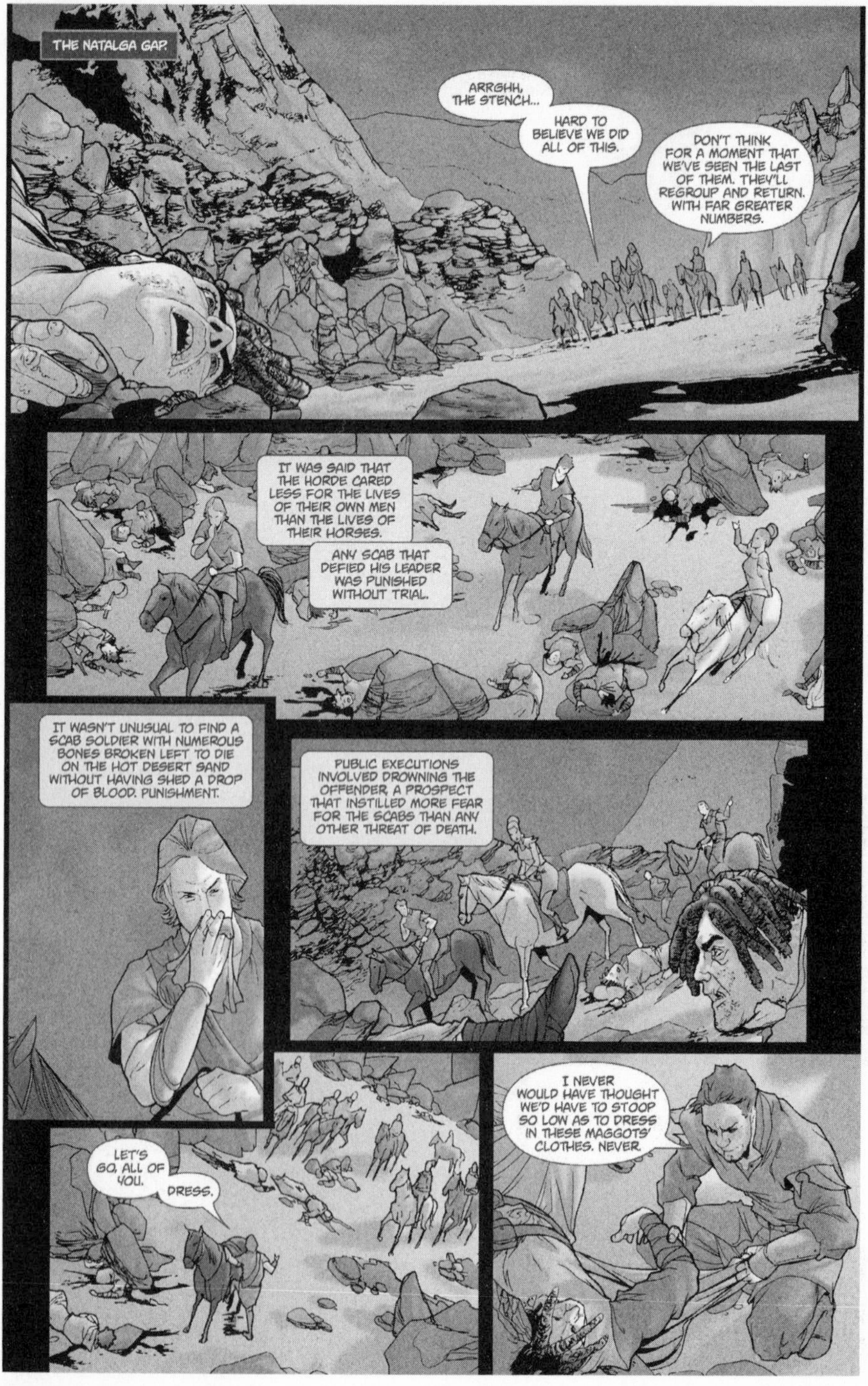
THE NATALGA GAP.
ARRGHH, THE STENCH...
HARD TO BELIEVE WE DID ALL OF THIS.
DON'T THINK FOR A MOMENT THAT WE'VE SEEN THE LAST OF THEM. THEY'LL REGROUP AND RETURN. WITH FAR GREATER NUMBERS.
IT WAS SAID THAT THE HORDE CARED LESS FOR THE LIVES OF THEIR OWN MEN THAN THE LIVES OF THEIR HORSES.
ANY SCAB THAT DEFIED HIS LEADER WAS PUNISHED WITHOUT TRIAL.
IT WASN'T UNUSUAL TO FIND A SCAB SOLDIER WITH NUMEROUS BONES BROKEN LEFT TO DIE ON THE HOT DESERT SAND WITHOUT HAVING SHED A DROP OF BLOOD. PUNISHMENT.
PUBLIC EXECUTIONS INVOLVED DROWNING THE OFFENDER, A PROSPECT THAT INSTILLED MORE FEAR FOR THE SCABS THAN ANY OTHER THREAT OF DEATH.
LET'S GO, ALL OF YOU.
DRESS.
I NEVER WOULD HAVE THOUGHT WE'D HAVE TO STOOP SO LOW AS TO DRESS IN THESE MAGGOTS' CLOTHES. NEVER.

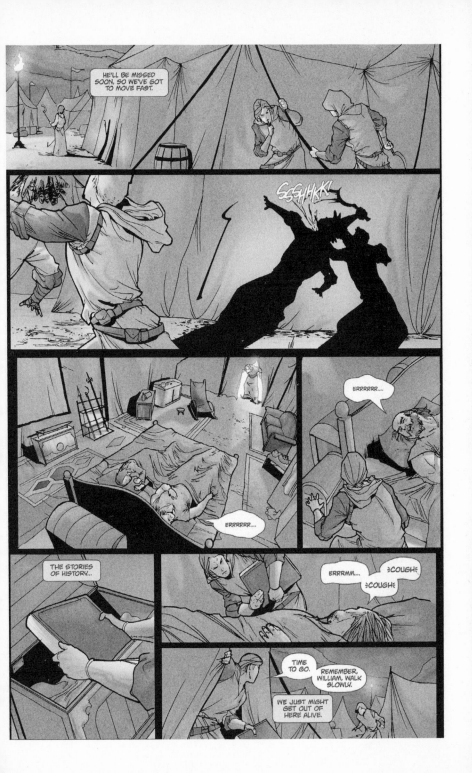

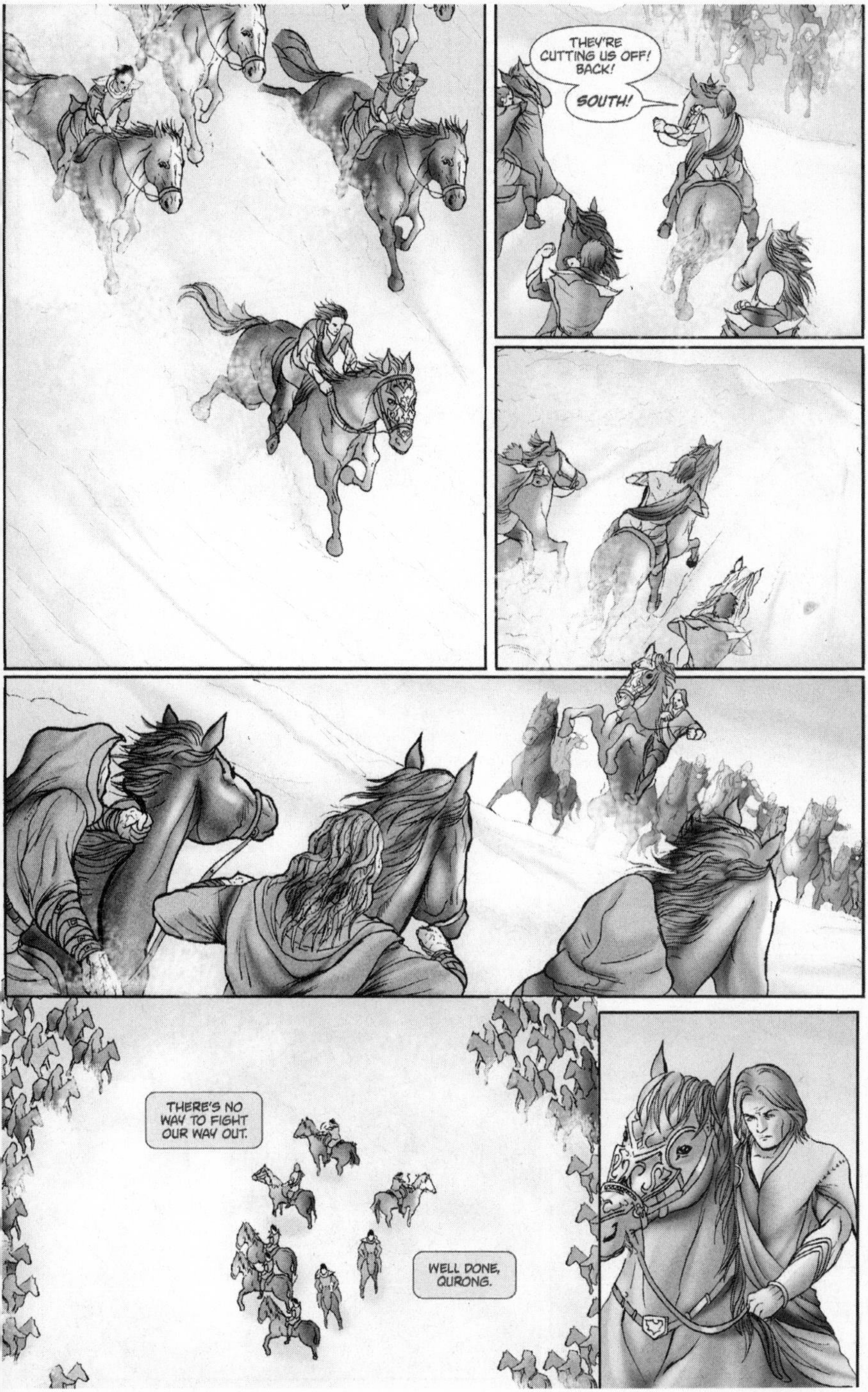
THEY'RE CUTTING US OFF! BACK!
SOUTH!
THERE'S NO WAY TO FIGHT OUR WAY OUT.
WELL DONE, QURONG.

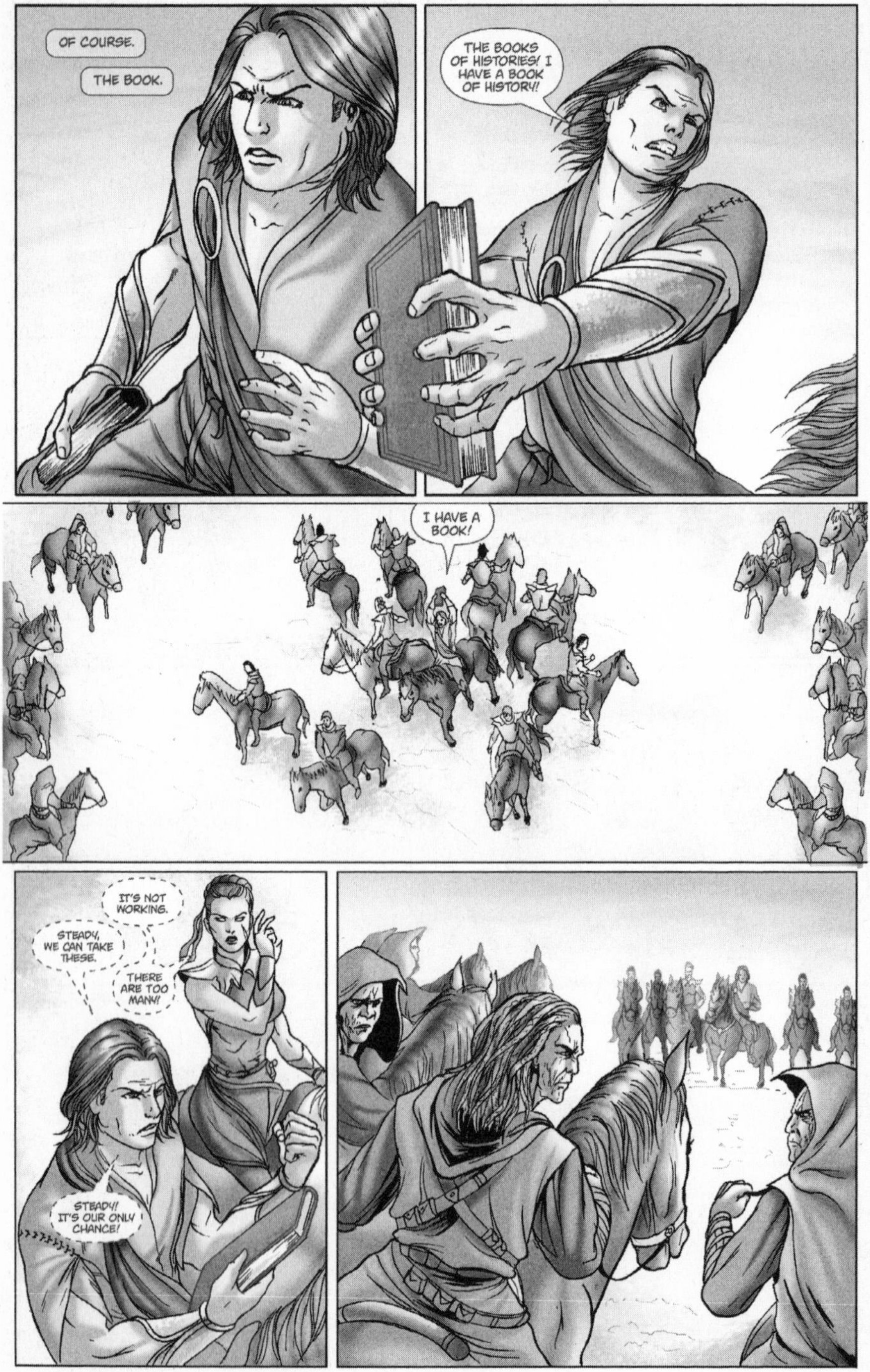
OF COURSE.
THE BOOK.
THE BOOKS OF HISTORIES! I HAVE A BOOK OF HISTORY!
I HAVE A BOOK!
IT'S NOT WORKING.
STEADY, WE CAN TAKE THESE.
THERE ARE TOO MANY!
STEADY! IT'S OUR ONLY CHANCE!

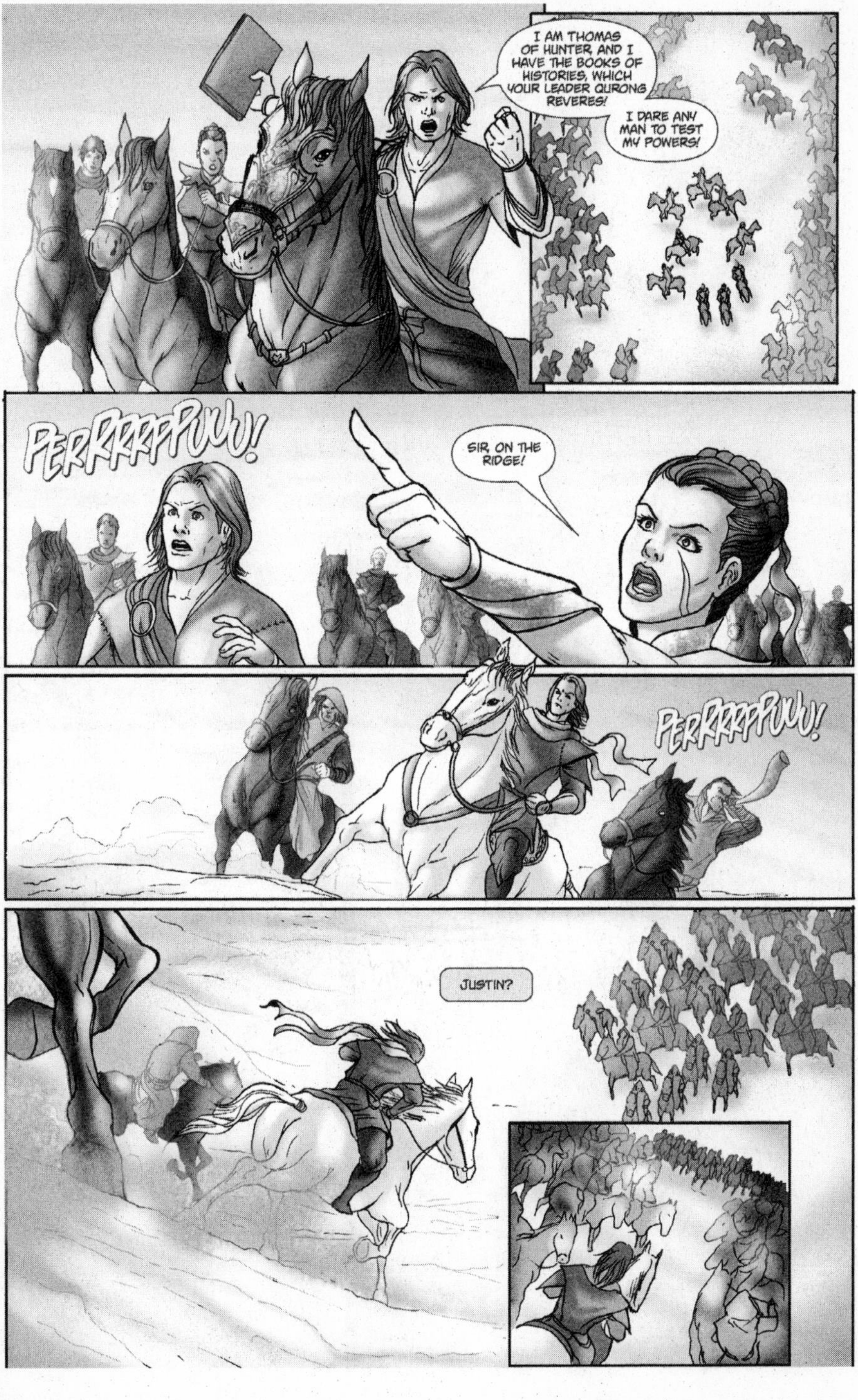
I AM THOMAS OF HUNTER AND I HAVE THE BOOKS OF HISTORIES, WHICH YOUR LEADER QURONG REVERES!
I DARE ANY MAN TO TEST MY POWERS!
PERRRRPPUUU!
SIR, ON THE RIDGE!
PERRRRPPUUU!
JUSTIN?

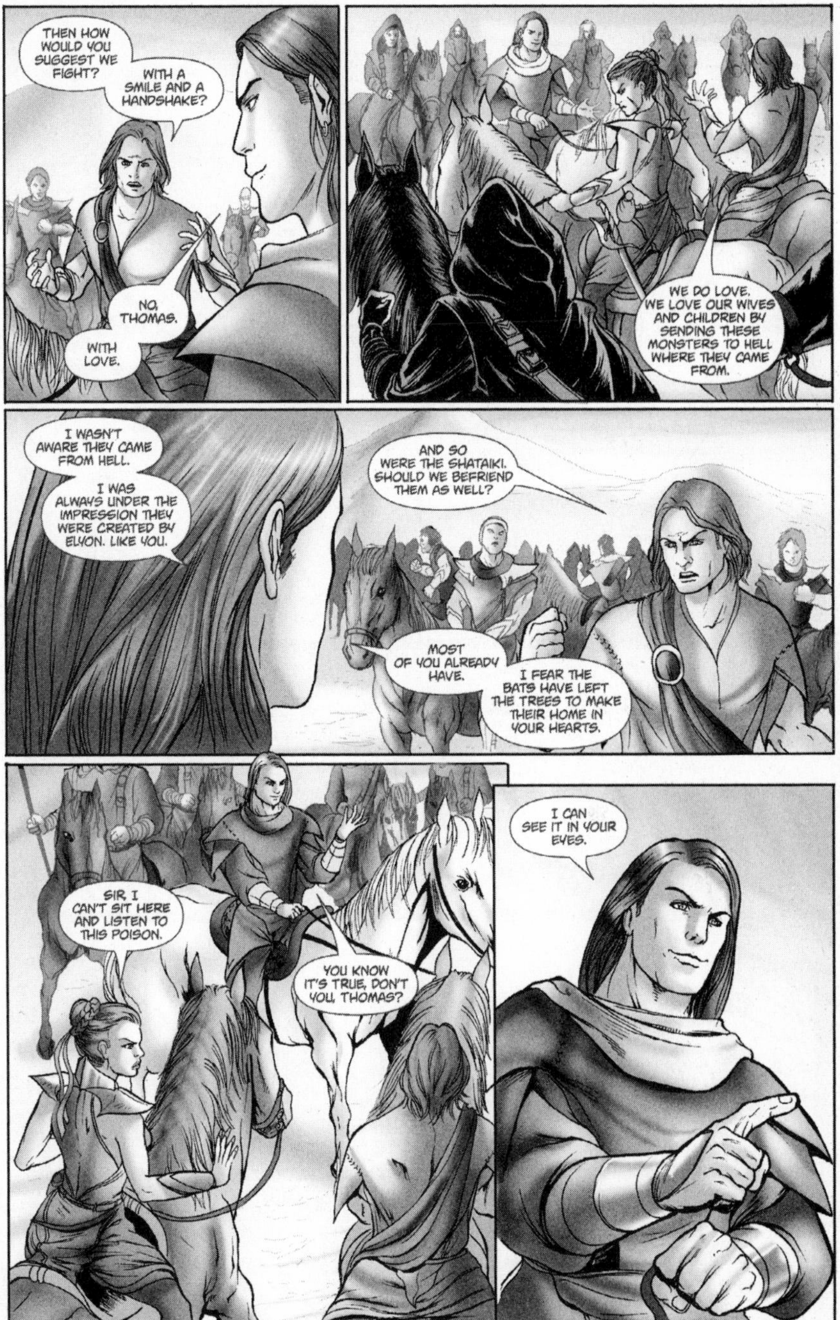
THEN HOW WOULD YOU SUGGEST WE FIGHT?
WITH A SMILE AND A HANDSHAKE?
NO, THOMAS.
WITH LOVE.
WE DO LOVE. WE LOVE OUR WIVES AND CHILDREN BY SENDING THESE MONSTERS TO HELL WHERE THEY CAME FROM.
I WASN'T AWARE THEY CAME FROM HELL.
I WAS ALWAYS UNDER THE IMPRESSION THEY WERE CREATED BY ELYON. LIKE YOU.
AND SO WERE THE SHATAIKI. SHOULD WE BEFRIEND THEM AS WELL?
MOST OF YOU ALREADY HAVE.
I FEAR THE BATS HAVE LEFT THE TREES TO MAKE THEIR HOME IN YOUR HEARTS.
SIR, I CAN'T SIT HERE AND LISTEN TO THIS POISON.
YOU KNOW IT'S TRUE, DON'T YOU, THOMAS?
I CAN SEE IT IN YOUR EYES.

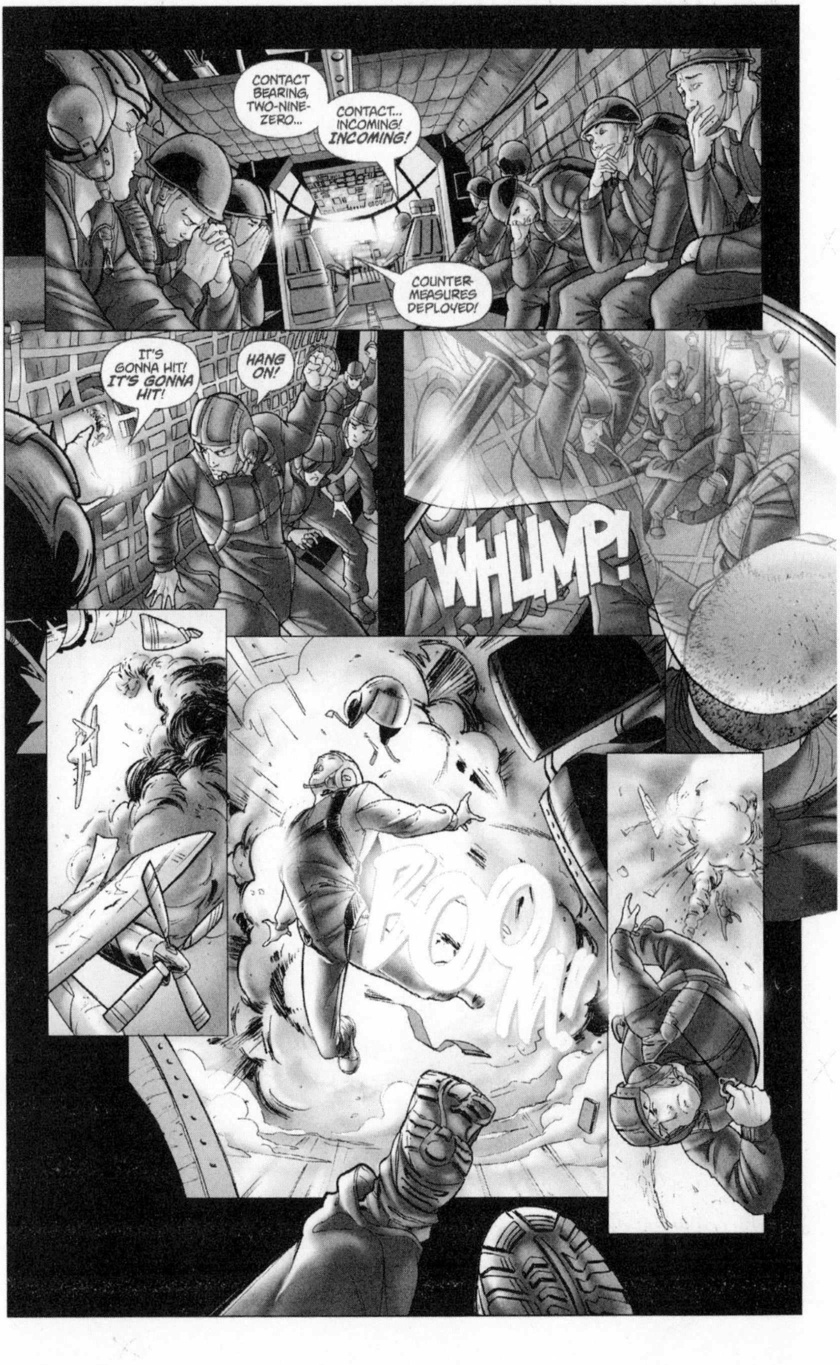
CONTACT BEARING, TWO-NINE-ZERO...
CONTACT... INCOMING! INCOMING!
COUNTER-MEASURES DEPLOYED!
IT'S GONNA HIT! IT'S GONNA HIT!
HANG ON!
WHUMP!
BOOM!

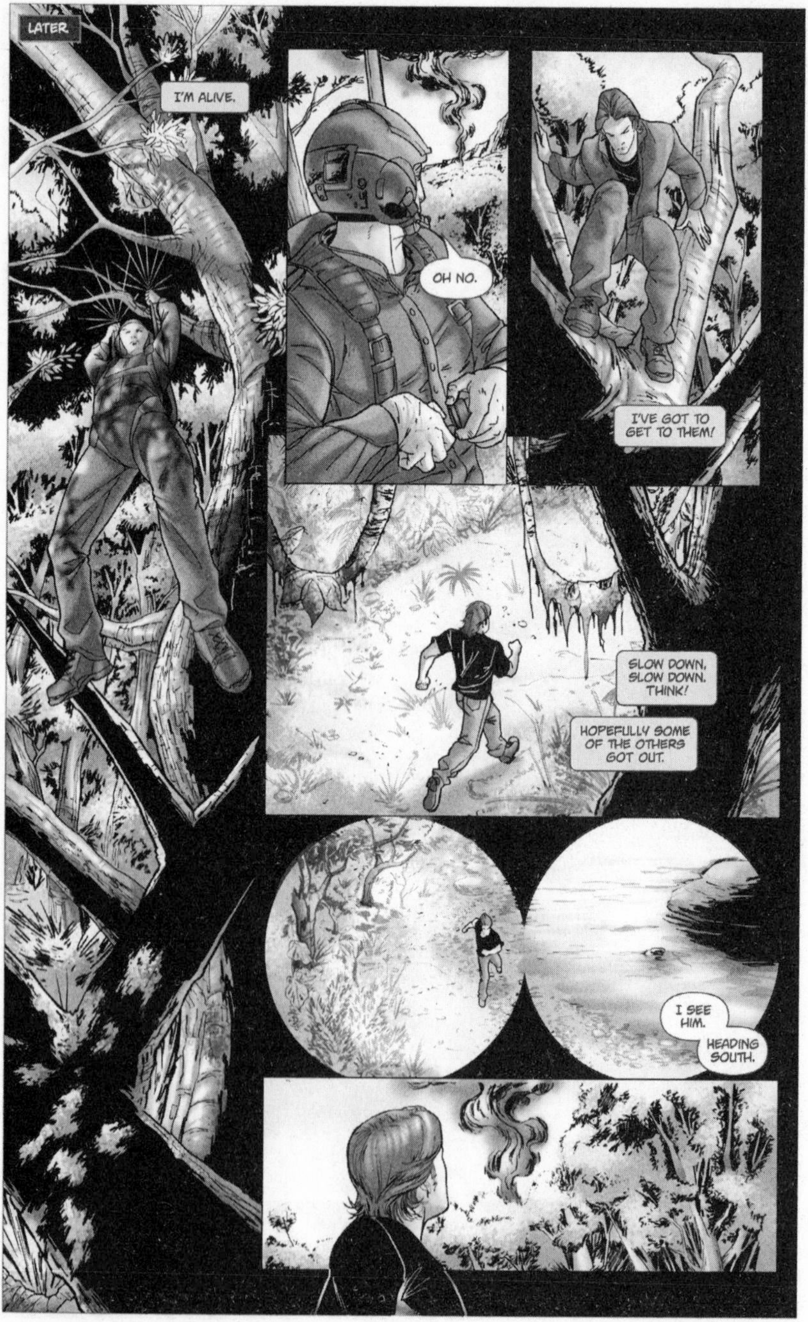
LATER
I'M ALIVE.
OH NO.
I'VE GOT TO GET TO THEM!
SLOW DOWN, SLOW DOWN. THINK!
HOPEFULLY SOME OF THE OTHERS GOT OUT.
I SEE HIM.
HEADING SOUTH.

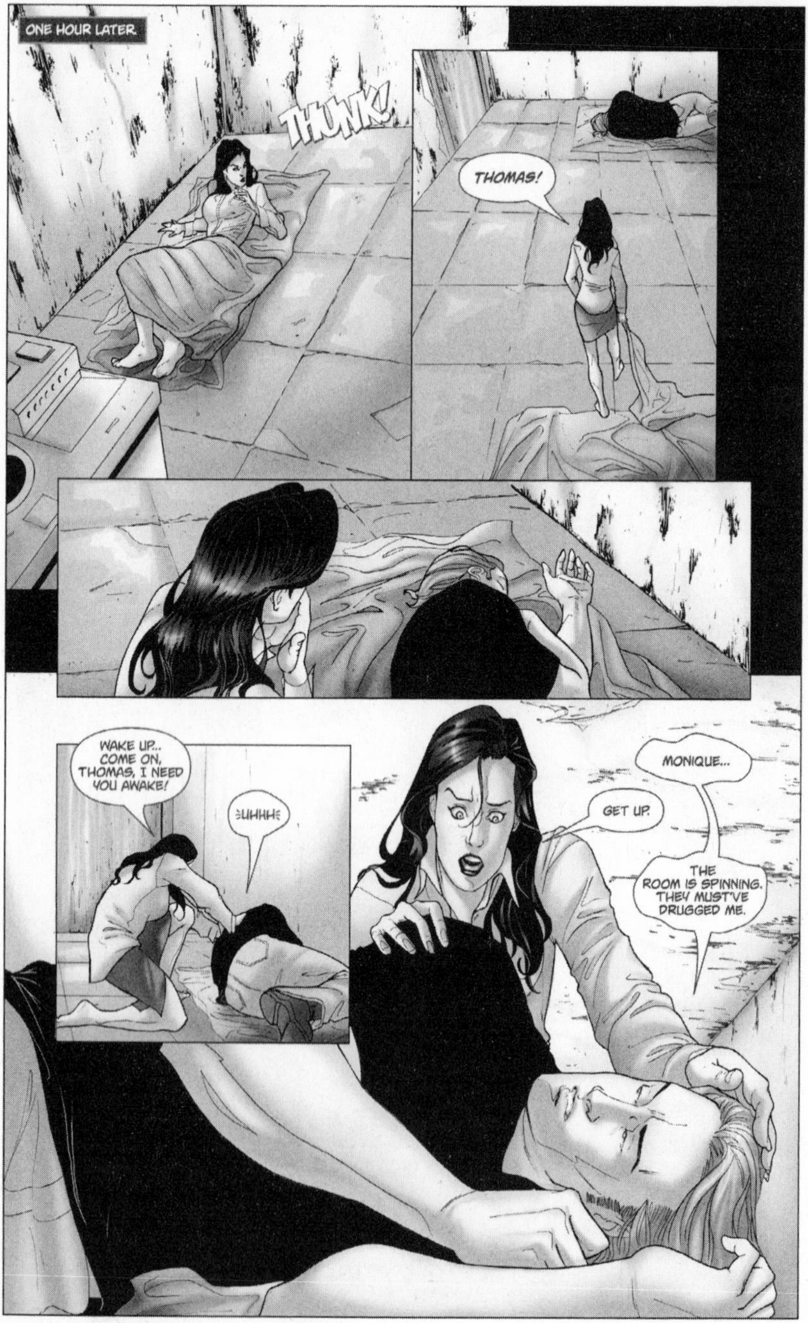
ONE HOUR LATER.
THUNK!
THOMAS!
WAKE UP... COME ON, THOMAS, I NEED YOU AWAKE!
UHHHH
GET UP.
MONIQUE...
THE ROOM IS SPINNING. THEY MUST'VE DRUGGED ME.

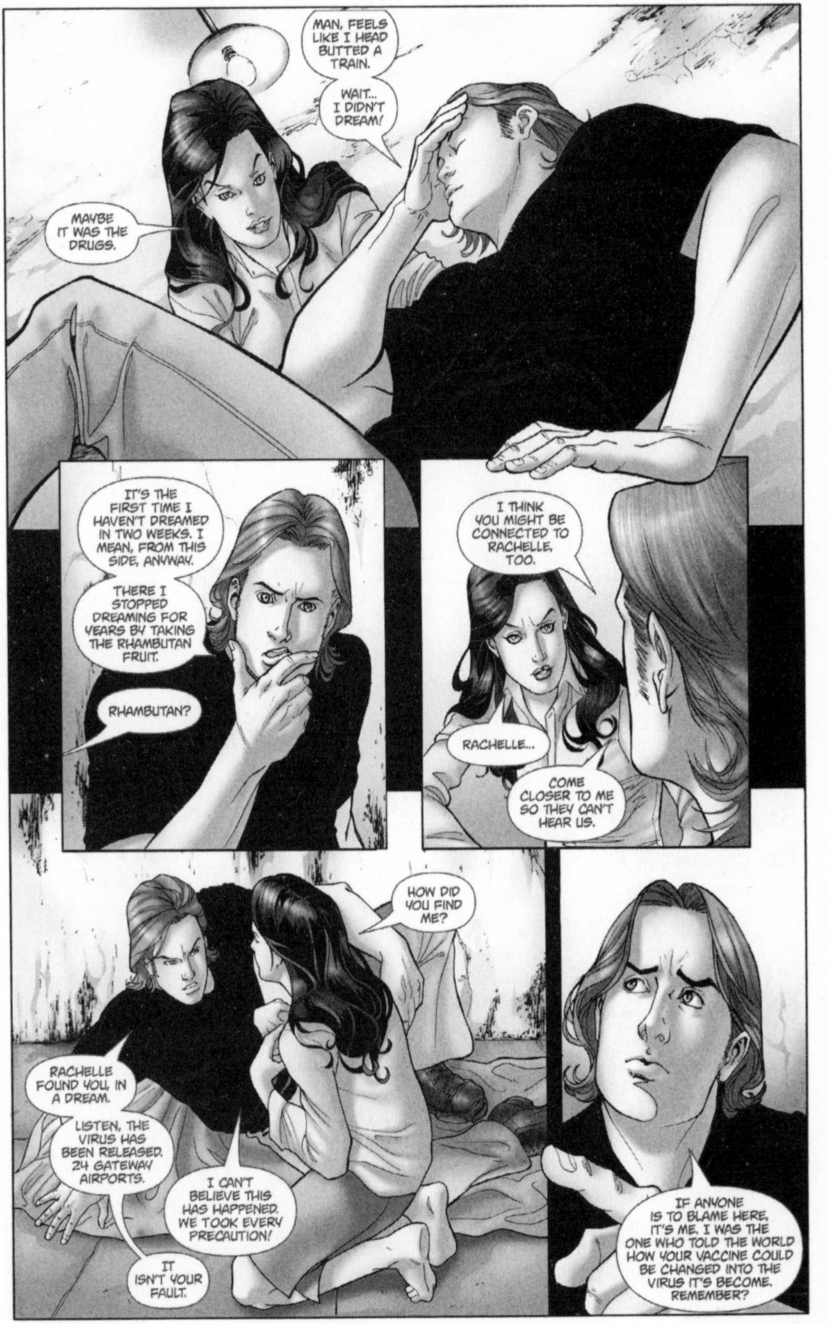
MAN, FEELS LIKE I HEAD BUTTED A TRAIN.
WAIT... I DIDN'T DREAM!
MAYBE IT WAS THE DRUGS.
IT'S THE FIRST TIME I HAVEN'T DREAMED IN TWO WEEKS. I MEAN, FROM THIS SIDE, ANYWAY.
THERE I STOPPED DREAMING FOR YEARS BY TAKING THE RHAMBUTAN FRUIT.
RHAMBUTAN?
I THINK YOU MIGHT BE CONNECTED TO RACHELLE, TOO.
RACHELLE...
COME CLOSER TO ME SO THEY CAN'T HEAR US.
HOW DID YOU FIND ME?
RACHELLE FOUND YOU, IN A DREAM.
LISTEN, THE VIRUS HAS BEEN RELEASED. 24 GATEWAY AIRPORTS.
I CAN'T BELIEVE THIS HAS HAPPENED. WE TOOK EVERY PRECAUTION!
IT ISN'T YOUR FAULT.
IF ANYONE IS TO BLAME HERE, IT'S ME. I WAS THE ONE WHO TOLD THE WORLD HOW YOUR VACCINE COULD BE CHANGED INTO THE VIRUS IT'S BECOME. REMEMBER?

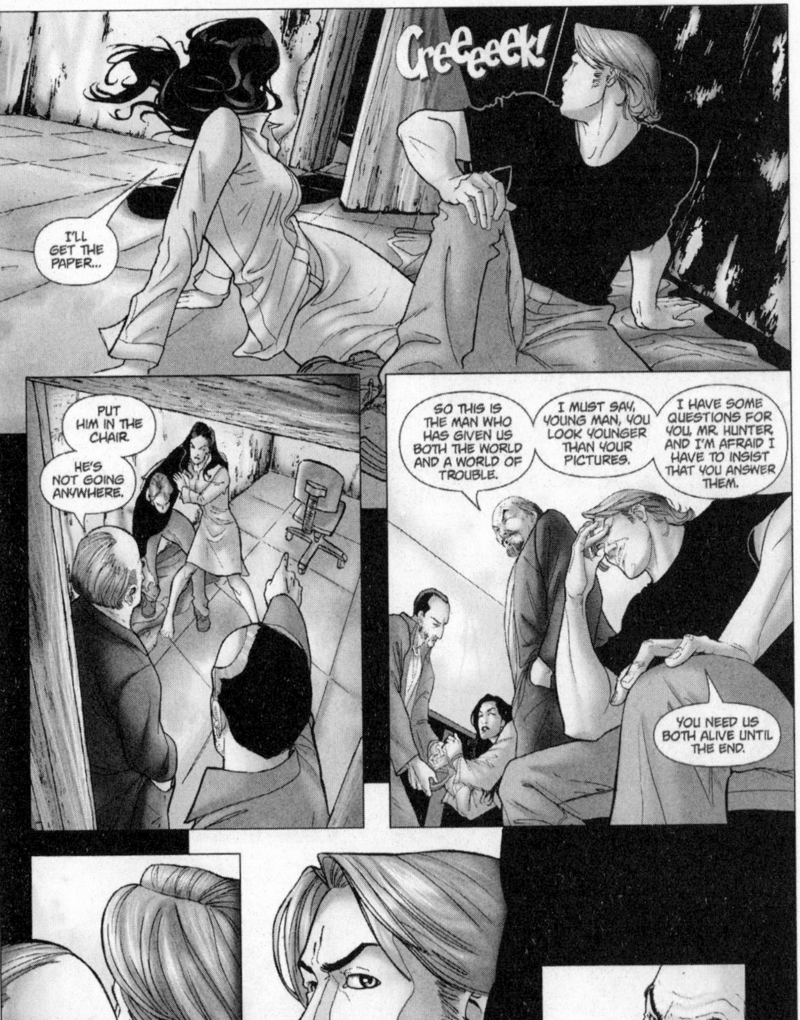
CREEEEEEK!
I'LL GET THE PAPER...
PUT HIM IN THE CHAIR.
HE'S NOT GOING ANYWHERE.
SO THIS IS THE MAN WHO HAS GIVEN US BOTH THE WORLD AND A WORLD OF TROUBLE.
I MUST SAY, YOUNG MAN, YOU LOOK YOUNGER THAN YOUR PICTURES.
I HAVE SOME QUESTIONS FOR YOU, MR. HUNTER AND I'M AFRAID I HAVE TO INSIST THAT YOU ANSWER THEM.
YOU NEED US BOTH ALIVE UNTIL THE END.
IS THAT SO?
ONLY A FOOL WOULD ELIMINATE THE TWO PEOPLE WHO MADE ALL OF THIS POSSIBLE WITH INFORMATION THEY ALONE HAD.
PERHAPS I AM A FOOL, THEN.
CARLOS. YOU MAY BEGIN.

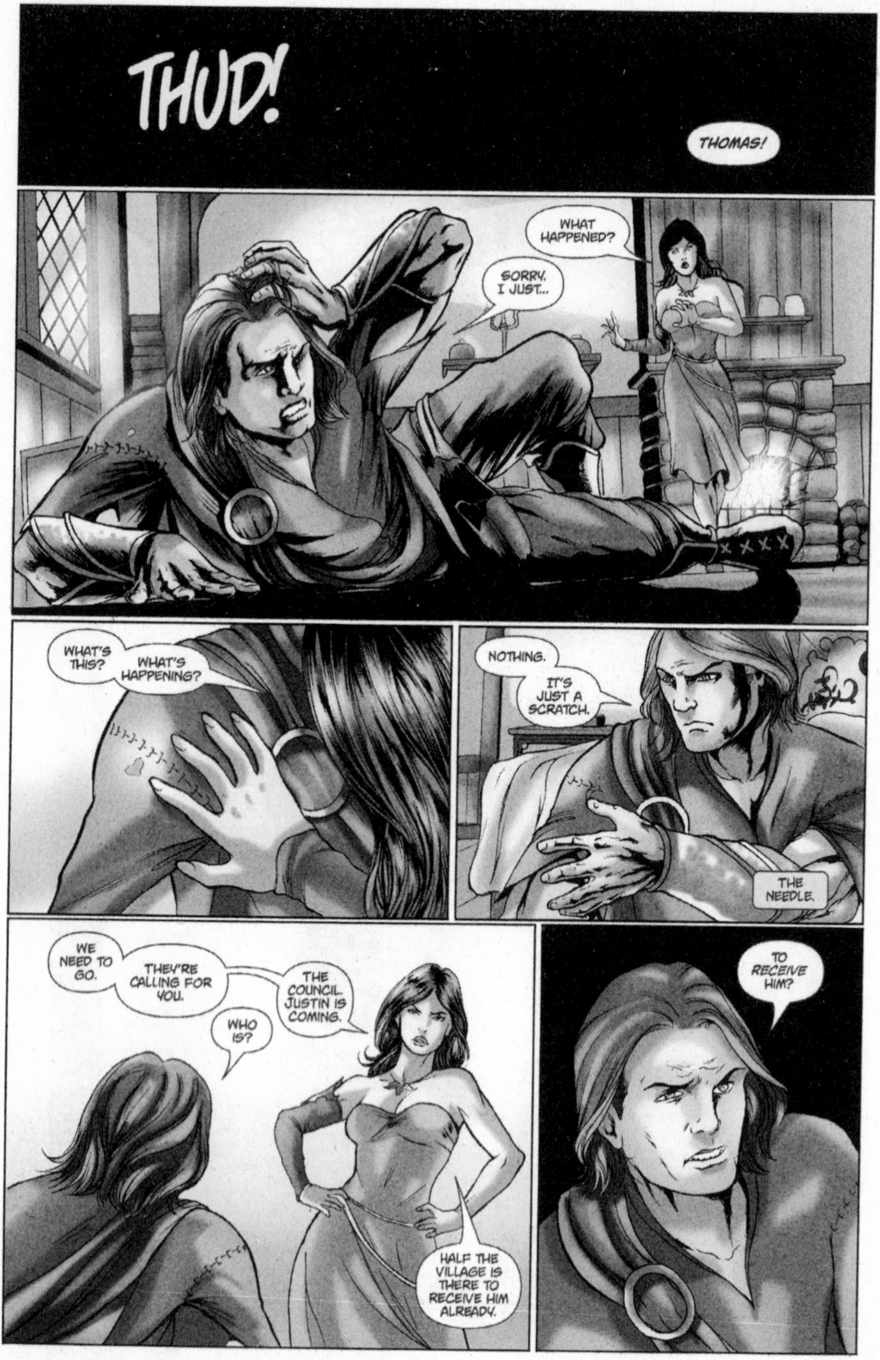
THUD!
THOMAS!
WHAT HAPPENED?
SORRY. I JUST...
WHAT'S THIS?
WHAT'S HAPPENING?
NOTHING.
IT'S JUST A SCRATCH.
THE NEEDLE.
WE NEED TO GO.
THEY'RE CALLING FOR YOU.
THE COUNCIL. JUSTIN IS COMING.
WHO IS?
HALF THE VILLAGE IS THERE TO RECEIVE HIM ALREADY.
TO RECEIVE HIM?

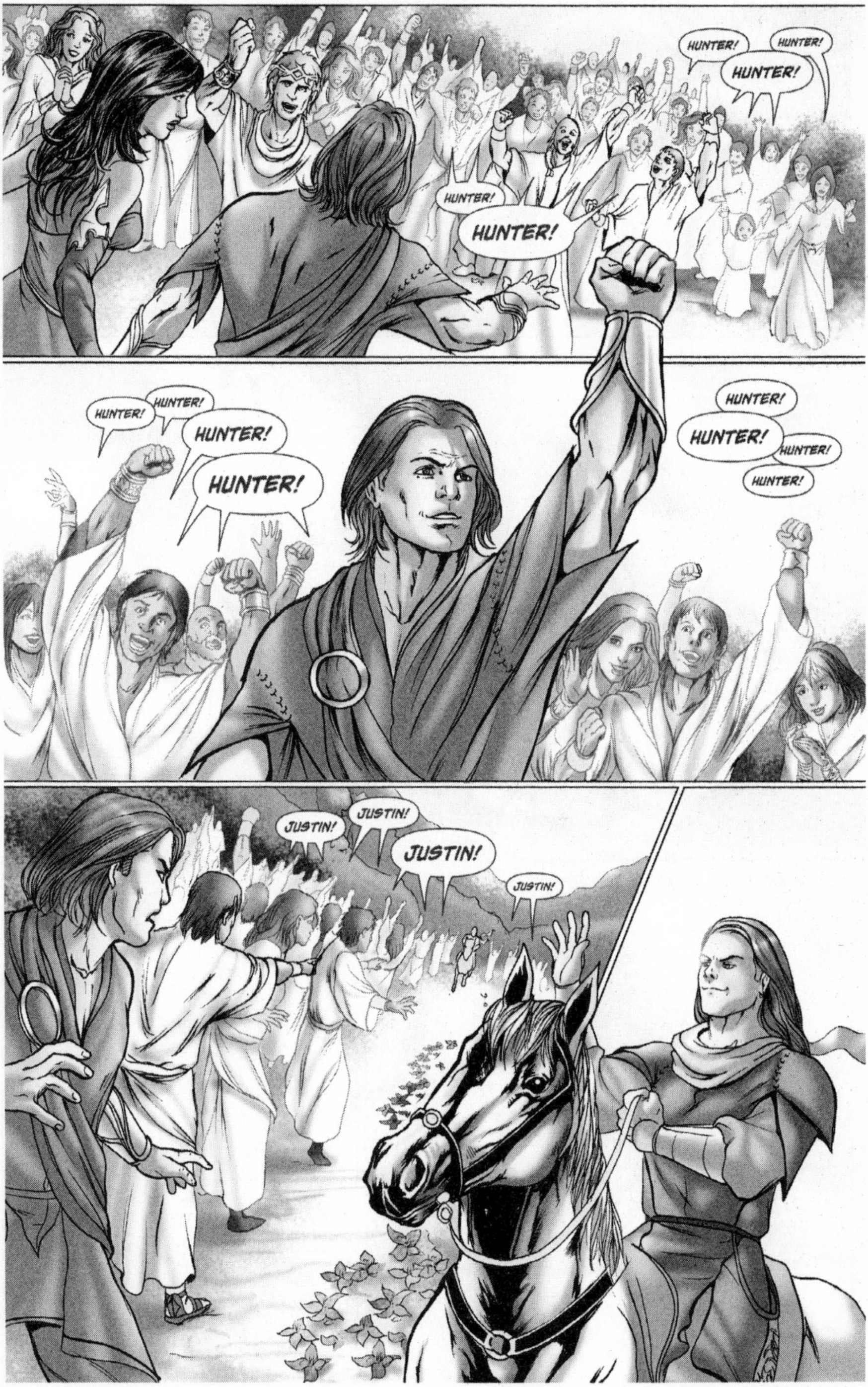
HUNTER!
HUNTER!
HUNTER!
HUNTER!
HUNTER!
HUNTER!
HUNTER!
HUNTER!
HUNTER!
HUNTER!
HUNTER!
HUNTER!
HUNTER!
JUSTIN!
JUSTIN!
JUSTIN!
JUSTIN!

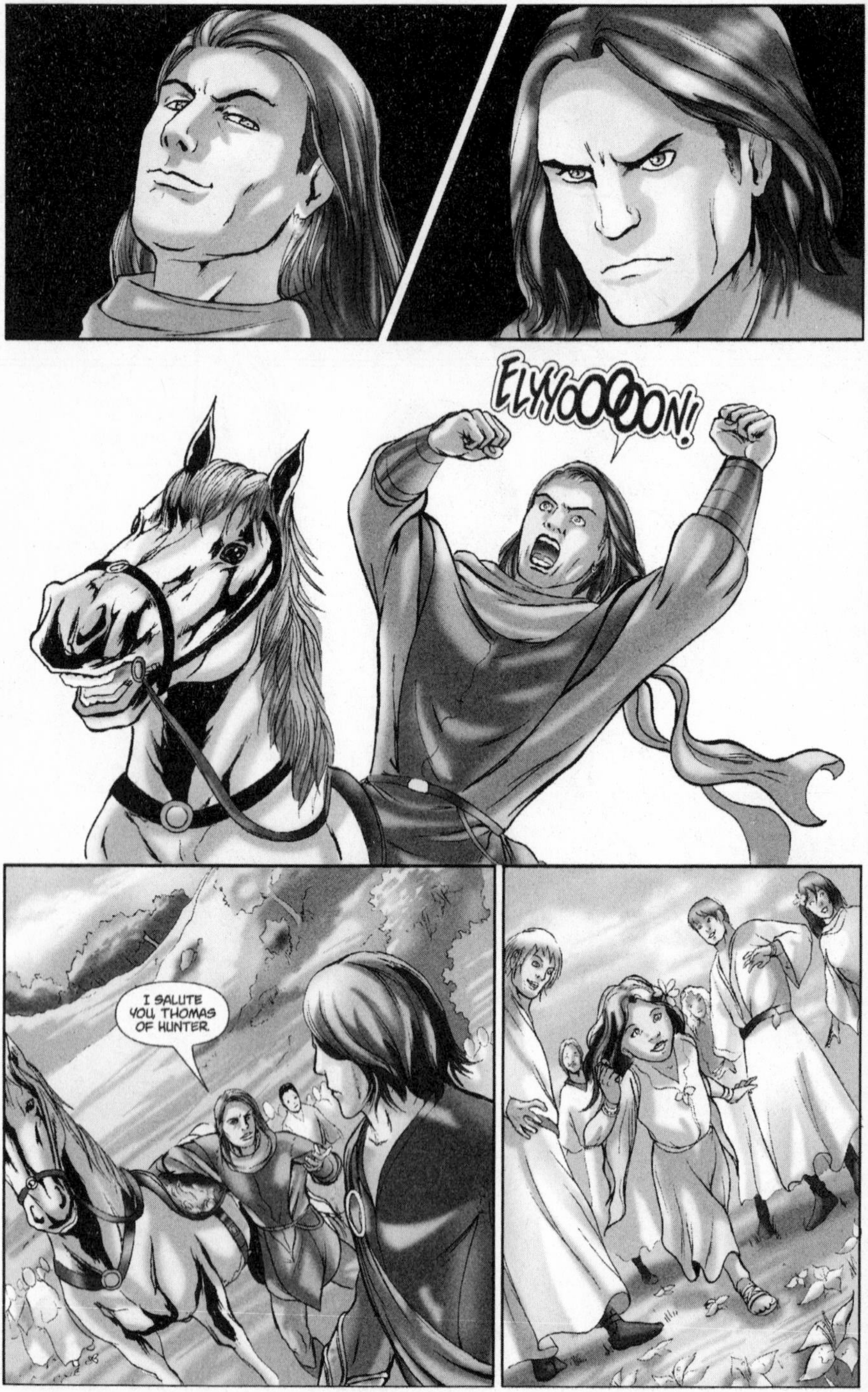
ELYYOOOOON!
I SALUTE YOU, THOMAS OF HUNTER.

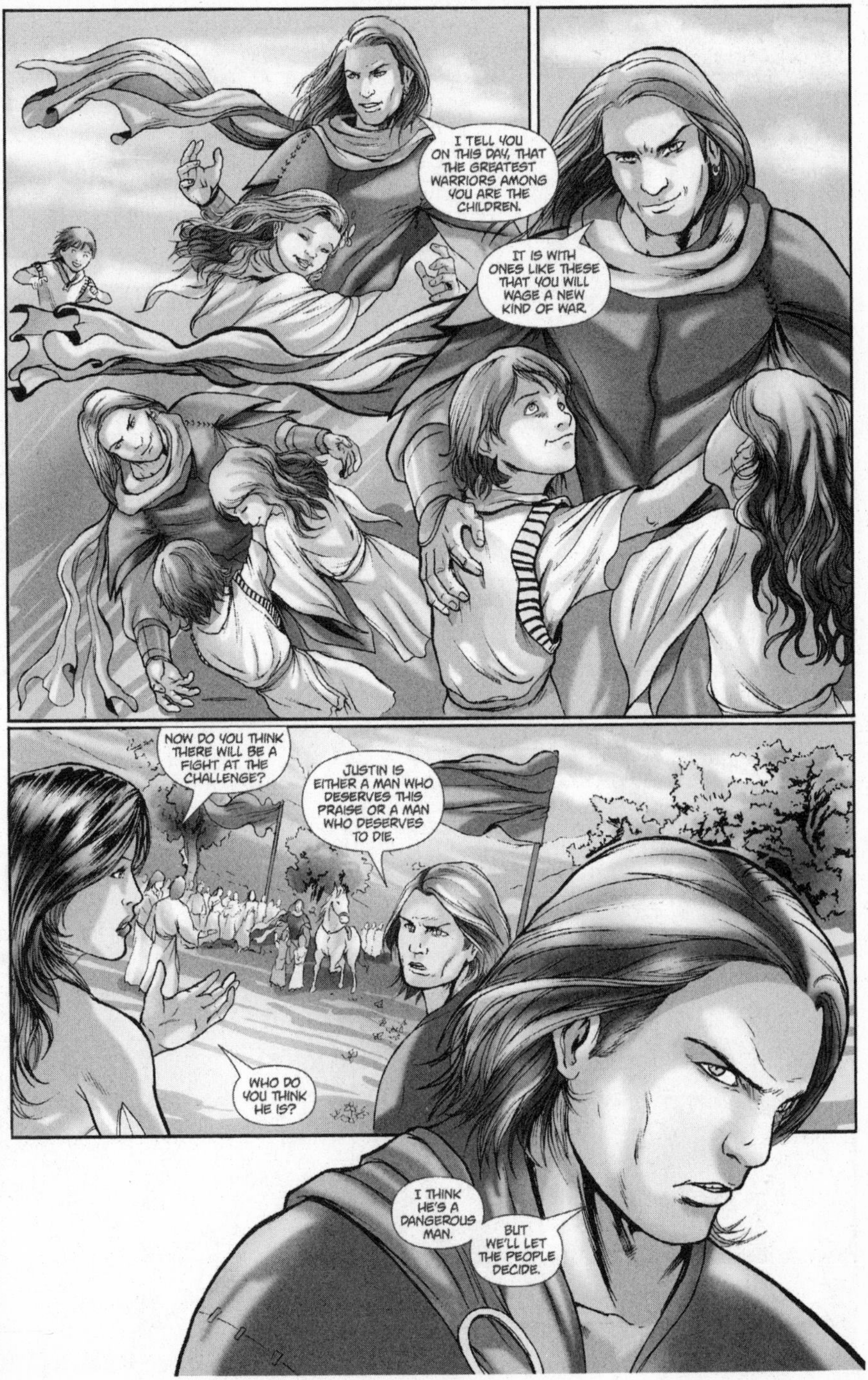
I TELL YOU ON THIS DAY, THAT THE GREATEST WARRIORS AMONG YOU ARE THE CHILDREN.
IT IS WITH ONES LIKE THESE THAT YOU WILL WAGE A NEW KIND OF WAR.
NOW DO YOU THINK THERE WILL BE A FIGHT AT THE CHALLENGE?
JUSTIN IS EITHER A MAN WHO DESERVES THIS PRAISE OR A MAN WHO DESERVES TO DIE.
WHO DO YOU THINK HE IS?
I THINK HE'S A DANGEROUS MAN.
BUT WE'LL LET THE PEOPLE DECIDE.

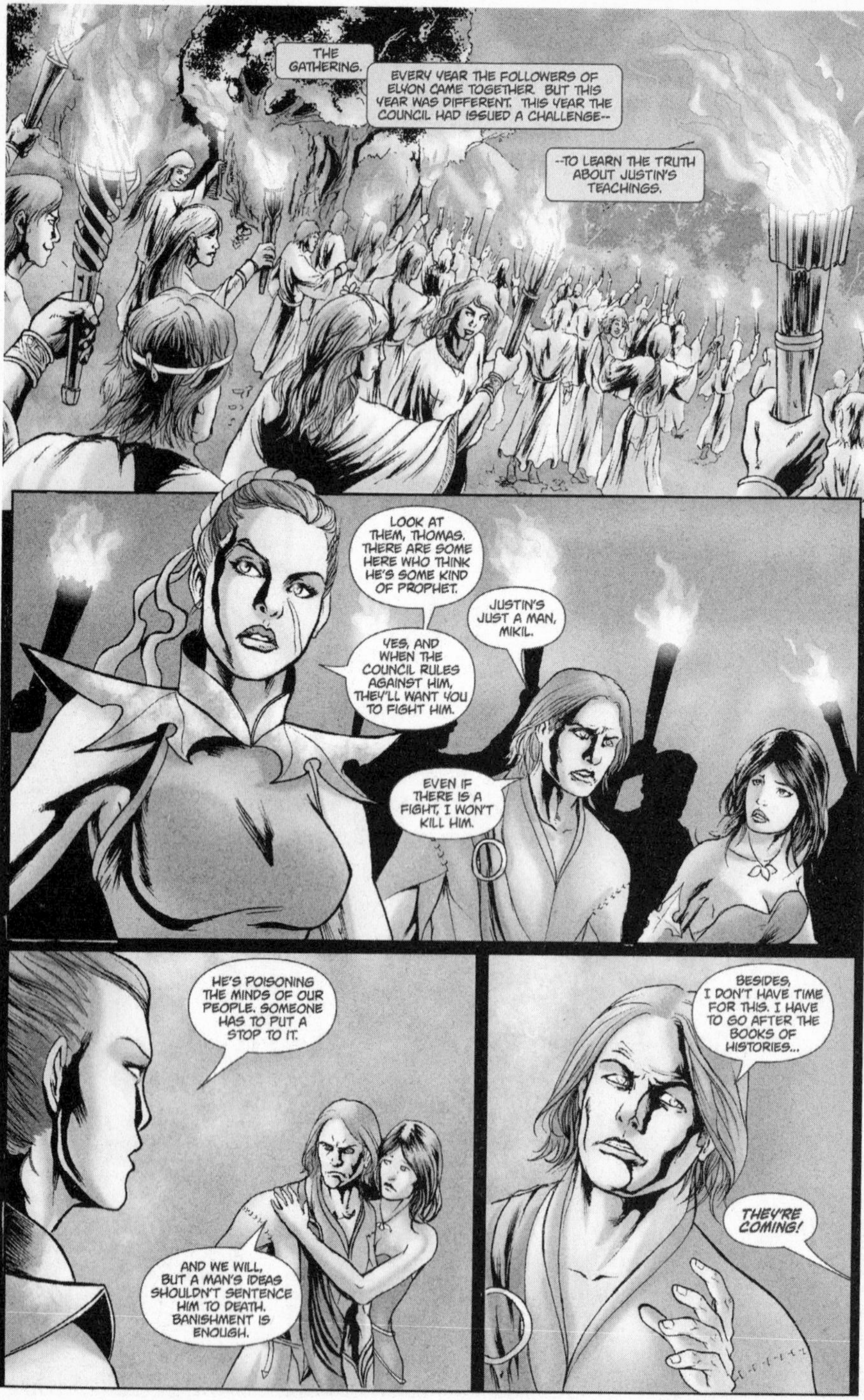
THE GATHERING.
EVERY YEAR THE FOLLOWERS OF ELYON CAME TOGETHER. BUT THIS YEAR WAS DIFFERENT. THIS YEAR THE COUNCIL HAD ISSUED A CHALLENGE--
--TO LEARN THE TRUTH ABOUT JUSTIN'S TEACHINGS.
LOOK AT THEM, THOMAS. THERE ARE SOME HERE WHO THINK HE'S SOME KIND OF PROPHET.
JUSTIN'S JUST A MAN, MIKIL.
YES, AND WHEN THE COUNCIL RULES AGAINST HIM, THEY'LL WANT YOU TO FIGHT HIM.
EVEN IF THERE IS A FIGHT, I WON'T KILL HIM.
HE'S POISONING THE MINDS OF OUR PEOPLE. SOMEONE HAS TO PUT A STOP TO IT.
AND WE WILL, BUT A MAN'S IDEAS SHOULDN'T SENTENCE HIM TO DEATH. BANISHMENT IS ENOUGH.
BESIDES, I DON'T HAVE TIME FOR THIS. I HAVE TO GO AFTER THE BOOKS OF HISTORIES...
THEY'RE COMING!

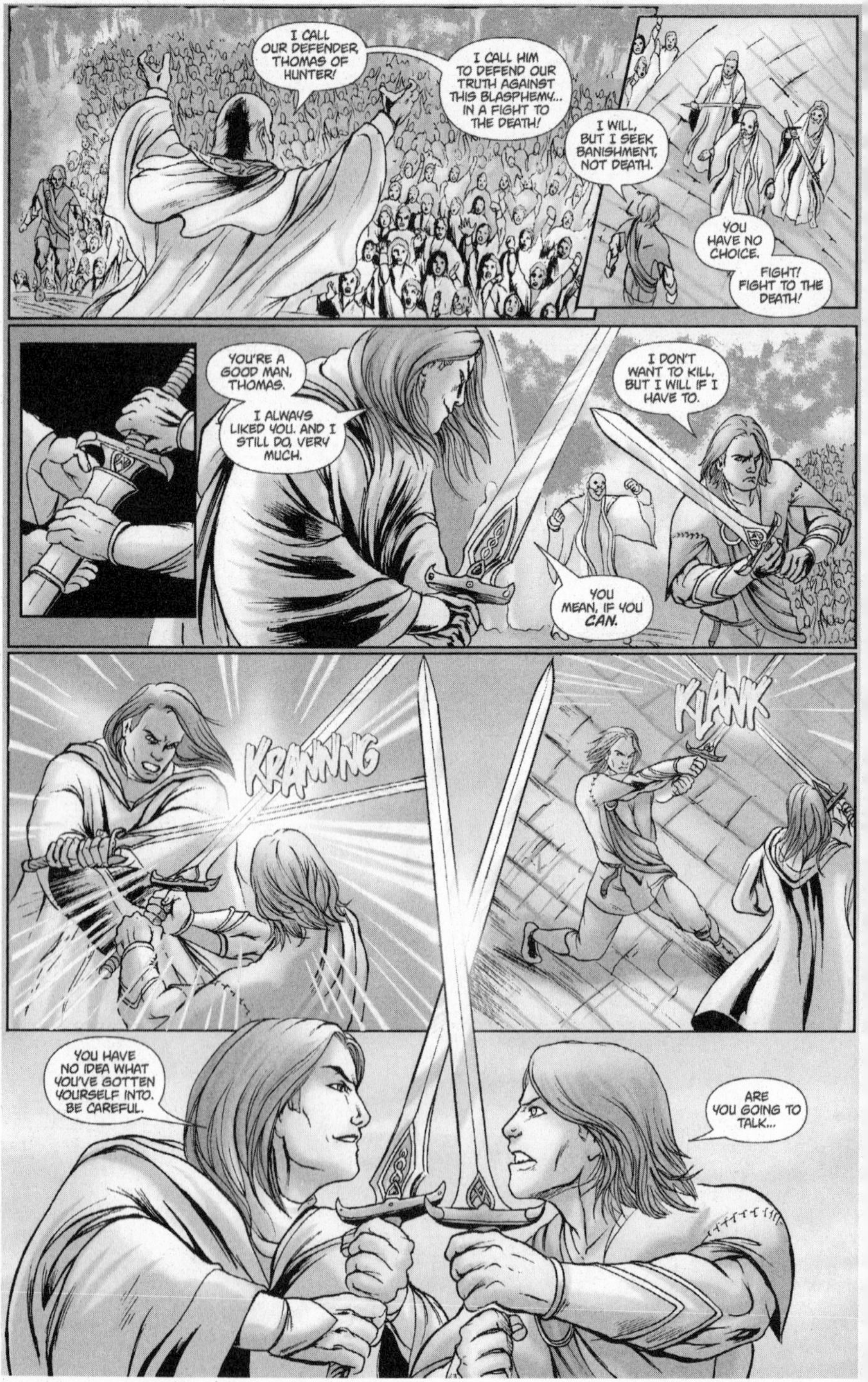
I CALL OUR DEFENDER, THOMAS OF HUNTER!
I CALL HIM TO DEFEND OUR TRUTH AGAINST THIS BLASPHEMY... IN A FIGHT TO THE DEATH!
I WILL, BUT I SEEK BANISHMENT, NOT DEATH.
YOU HAVE NO CHOICE.
FIGHT! FIGHT TO THE DEATH!
YOU'RE A GOOD MAN, THOMAS.
I ALWAYS LIKED YOU. AND I STILL DO, VERY MUCH.
I DON'T WANT TO KILL, BUT I WILL IF I HAVE TO.
YOU MEAN, IF YOU *CAN*.
KRANNNG
KLANK
YOU HAVE NO IDEA WHAT YOU'VE GOTTEN YOURSELF INTO. BE CAREFUL.
ARE YOU GOING TO TALK...

MONIQUE?

NO. NOT MONIQUE.

RACHELLE.

WHO HAD CRIED HERSELF TO SLEEP LAST NIGHT AFTER LEARNING THE TRUTH ABOUT HER BROTHER, JOHAN.

MIKIL! WAKE UP!

THOMAS?

HURRY, WE HAVE BUSINESS!

HAVE THE SCOUTS REPORTED IN?

NO. I'LL TELL YOU ON THE WAY.

WHY ARE WE HEADED TO THE STABLES?

LISTEN TO ME. WHAT WOULD YOU SAY IF I TOLD YOU JUSTIN MIGHT HAVE BETRAYAL IN MIND?

I KNEW IT! HE'LL BE THE END OF THE FOREST! BUT, HOW DO YOU KNOW?

I DREAMED.

OF WHAT?

FOR WHAT? NEGOTIATION? NO, THOMAS! NO PEACE!

OF WHAT I OVERHEARD IN QURONG'S TENT. WE NEED TO FIND MARTYN.

NO. I'M THINKING THAT MARTYN WILL LISTEN TO ANOTHER PROPOSAL. WE NEED TO TURN THIS BETRAYAL AGAINST JUSTIN, USE IT TO OUR ADVANTAGE.

AND I KNOW JUST HOW TO DO IT.

GENERAL MARTYN'S TENT.

COMING HERE WAS EITHER VERY SMART OR VERY STUPID. WHY HAVE YOU COME?

AM I?

I KNOW YOU'RE CONSPIRING WITH JUSTIN AND QURONG AGAINST THE FOREST PEOPLE.

YOU WILL USE JUSTIN TO OFFER OUR PEOPLE PEACE, THEN BETRAY US.

A SMALL PRICE TO PAY FOR PEACE.

OR CONQUEST.

IT DOESN'T HAVE TO BE THIS WAY, JOHAN. PEACE MAY NOT BE POSSIBLE, BUT A TRUCE IS.

AS JUSTIN PROPOSED. A TRUCE.

I COULD HAVE YOU KILLED FOR SUCH WORDS. YOU'RE SUGGESTING A REVOLT AGAINST QURONG, MY FATHER.

THAT WILL END IN RIVERS OF BLOODSHED, MOSTLY YOUR PEOPLE'S. THE ONLY WAY TO A TRUCE IS FOR YOU TO LEAD THE HORDE INSTEAD OF QURONG.

HE IS. SINCE THE TIME HE WAS CALLED TANIS, HE HAS BEEN A FATHER TO ME.

I KNEW YOUR FATHER, AND QURONG IS NOT HIM.

I WILL ENSURE YOUR SAFE PASSAGE INTO THE FOREST WITH QURONG AND JUSTIN. BRING A THOUSAND OF YOUR BEST WARRIORS IF YOU MUST.

BEFORE THE PEOPLE, YOU WILL EXPOSE THE BETRAYAL OF JUSTIN AND QURONG, AND I WILL SWEAR YOU SAY THE TRUTH. WE WILL CONDEMN QURONG TO DEATH, AND YOU WILL RULE.

TANIS? QURONG IS TANIS?!

YOU THINK I'M FOOLISH ENOUGH TO WALK INTO A TRAP? QURONG WILL NEVER ALLOW ME TO ACCOMPANY HIM. IT IS TOO RISKY.

HE WILL IF I STAY HERE AS A GUARANTEE OF HIS SAFETY.

YOUR PLAN IS TREASONOUS. I'M NOT A MAN WHO ENTERTAINS TREASON.

DO IT YOUR WAY AND MANY WILL DIE, AND THERE MAY NOT BE ENOUGH OF YOUR PEOPLE TO RULE.

I ALREADY KNOW YOU PLAN TO BETRAY THE FOREST PEOPLE. YOU WILL PROMISE PEACE, THEN YOU WILL INVADE THEM.

I WILL CONSIDER IT.

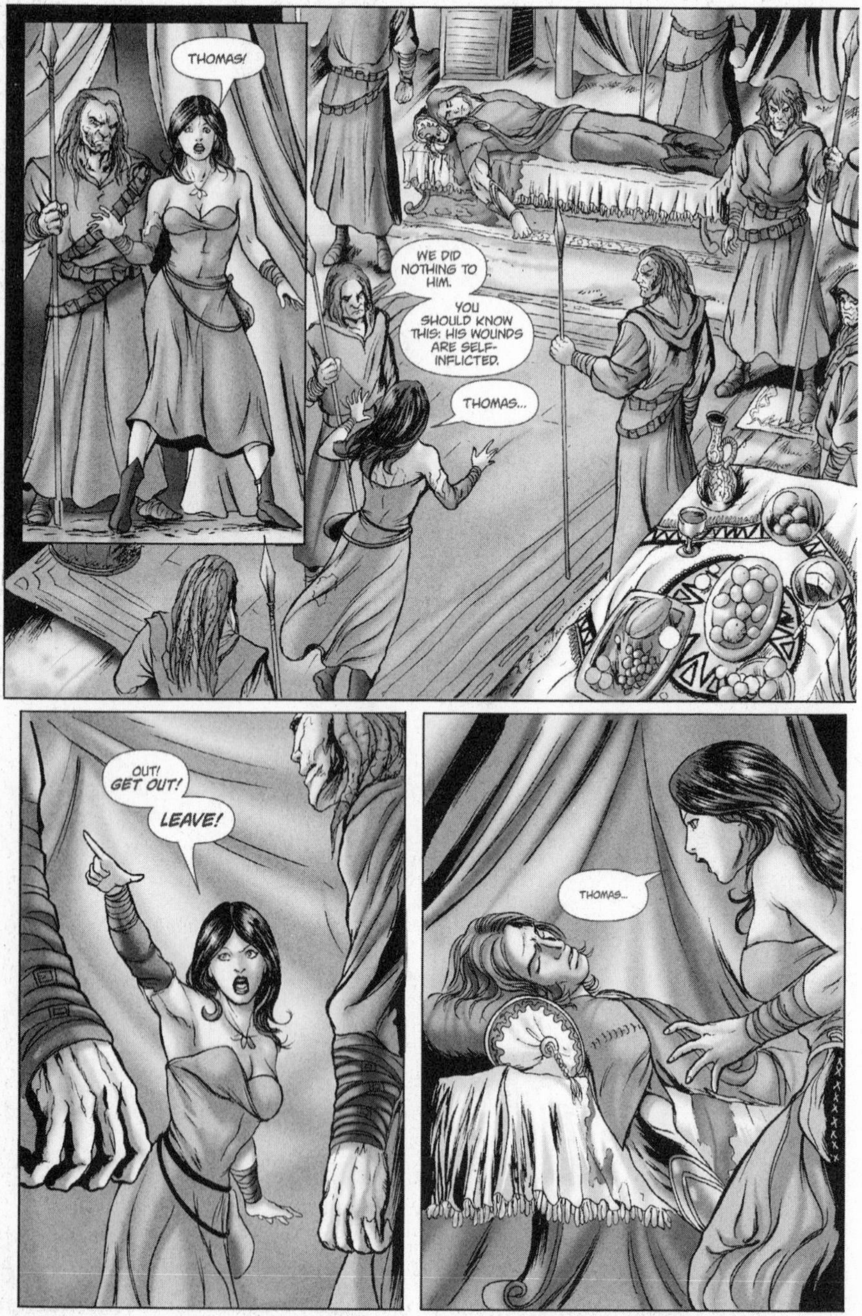
THOMAS!
WE DID NOTHING TO HIM.
YOU SHOULD KNOW THIS: HIS WOUNDS ARE SELF-INFLICTED.
THOMAS...
OUT! GET OUT!
LEAVE!
THOMAS...

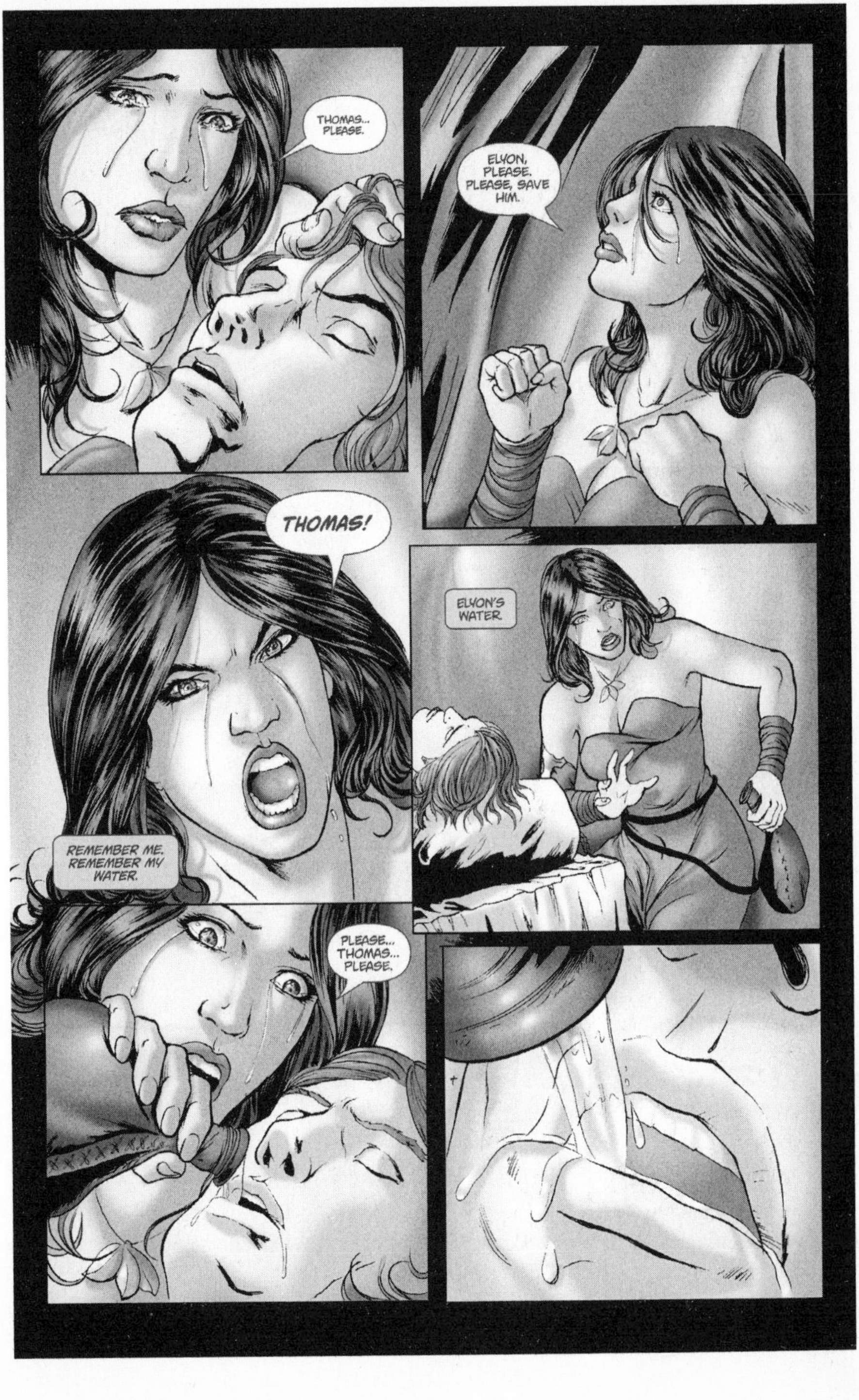
THOMAS... PLEASE.
ELYON, PLEASE. PLEASE, SAVE HIM.
THOMAS!
REMEMBER ME. REMEMBER MY WATER.
ELYON'S WATER.
PLEASE... THOMAS... PLEASE.

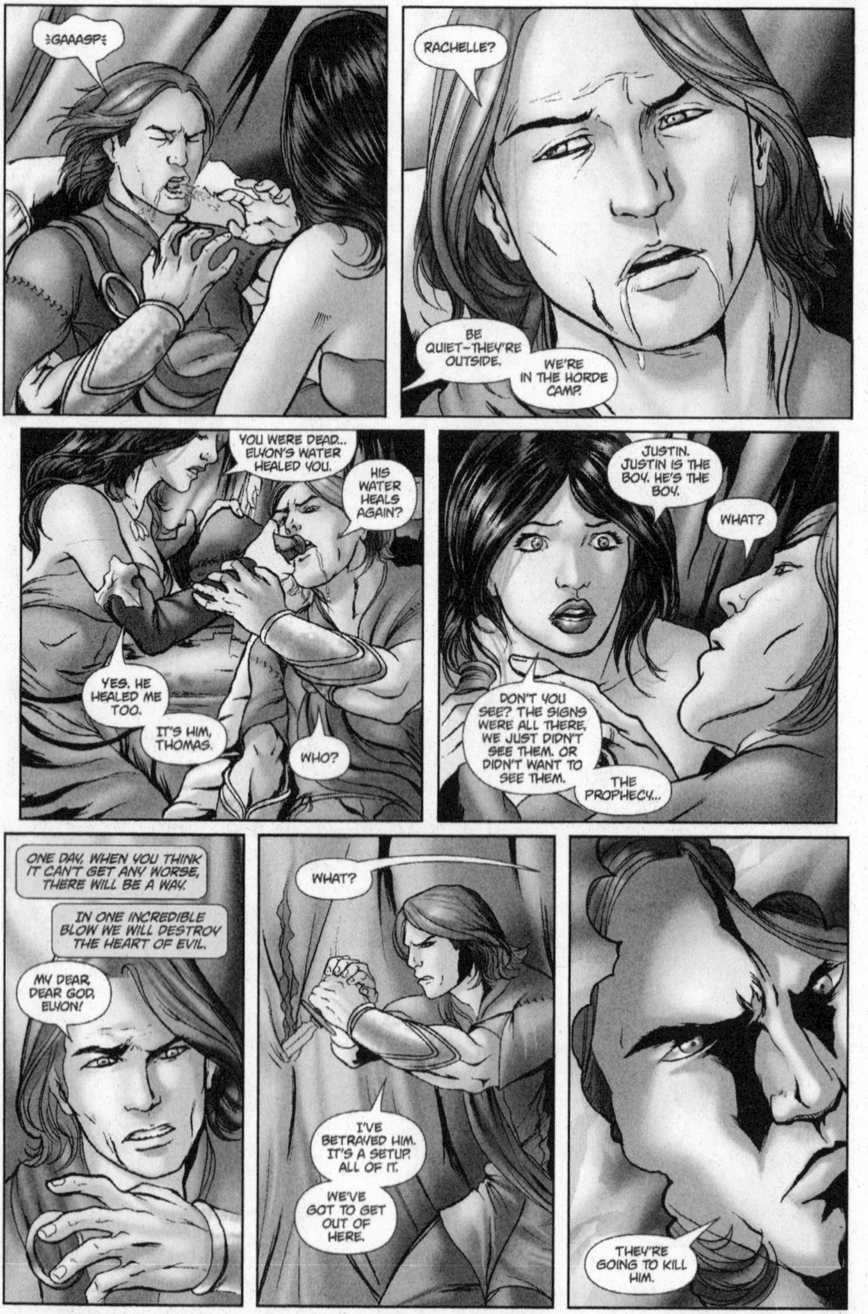
GAAASP
RACHELLE?
BE QUIET–THEY'RE OUTSIDE.
WE'RE IN THE HORDE CAMP.
YOU WERE DEAD... ELYON'S WATER HEALED YOU.
HIS WATER HEALS AGAIN?
YES. HE HEALED ME TOO.
IT'S HIM, THOMAS.
WHO?
JUSTIN. JUSTIN IS THE BOY. HE'S THE BOY.
WHAT?
DON'T YOU SEE? THE SIGNS WERE ALL THERE, WE JUST DIDN'T SEE THEM. OR DIDN'T WANT TO SEE THEM.
THE PROPHECY...
ONE DAY, WHEN YOU THINK IT CAN'T GET ANY WORSE, THERE WILL BE A WAY.
IN ONE INCREDIBLE BLOW WE WILL DESTROY THE HEART OF EVIL.
MY DEAR, DEAR GOD, ELYON!
WHAT?
I'VE BETRAYED HIM. IT'S A SETUP. ALL OF IT.
WE'VE GOT TO GET OUT OF HERE.
THEY'RE GOING TO KILL HIM.

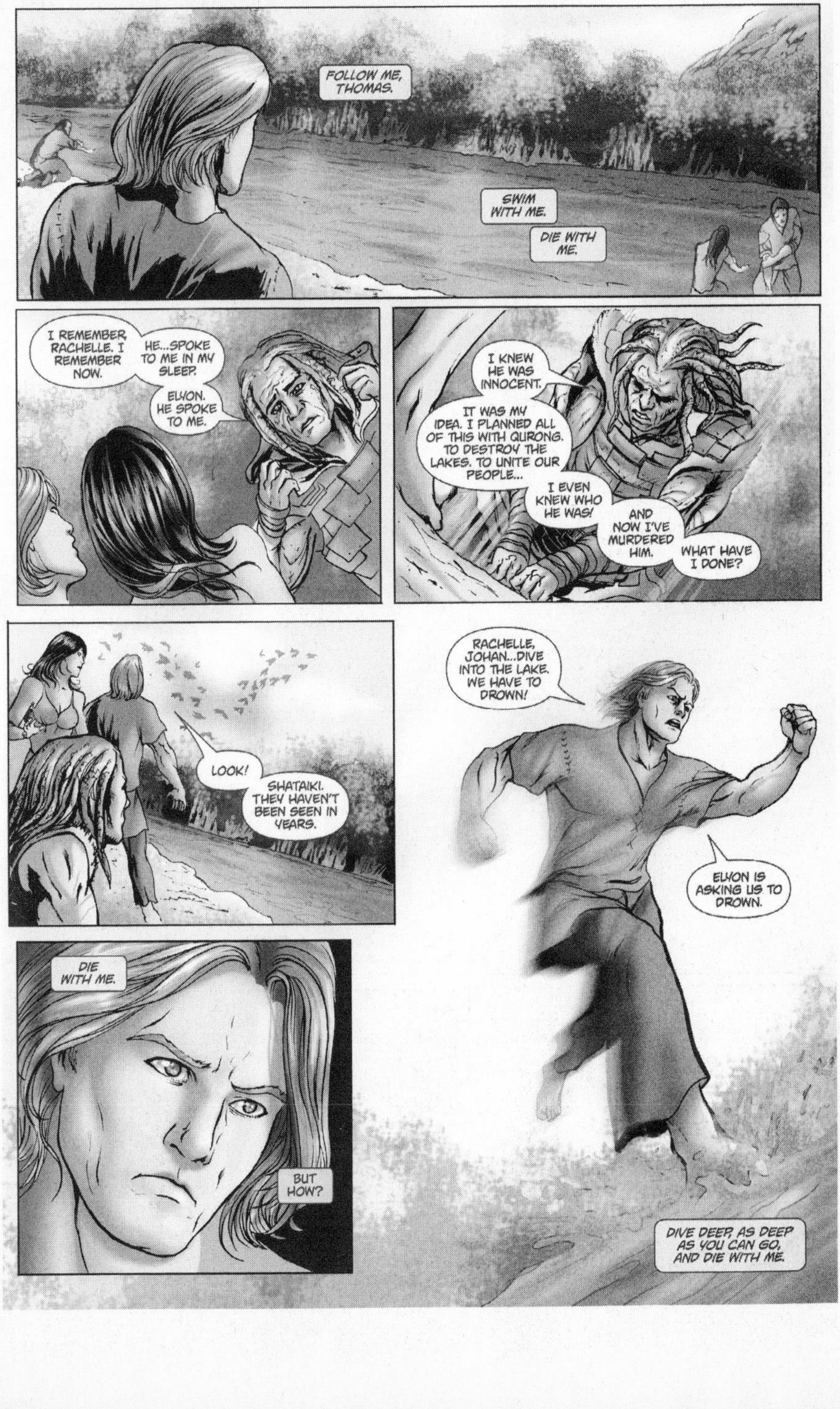
FOLLOW ME, THOMAS.
SWIM WITH ME.
DIE WITH ME.
I REMEMBER, RACHELLE. I REMEMBER NOW.
HE...SPOKE TO ME IN MY SLEEP.
ELYON. HE SPOKE TO ME.
I KNEW HE WAS INNOCENT.
IT WAS MY IDEA. I PLANNED ALL OF THIS WITH QURONG. TO DESTROY THE LAKES. TO UNITE OUR PEOPLE...
I EVEN KNEW WHO HE WAS!
AND NOW I'VE MURDERED HIM.
WHAT HAVE I DONE?
LOOK!
SHATAIKI. THEY HAVEN'T BEEN SEEN IN YEARS.
RACHELLE, JOHAN...DIVE INTO THE LAKE. WE HAVE TO DROWN!
ELYON IS ASKING US TO DROWN.
DIE WITH ME.
BUT HOW?
DIVE DEEP, AS DEEP AS YOU CAN GO, AND DIE WITH ME.

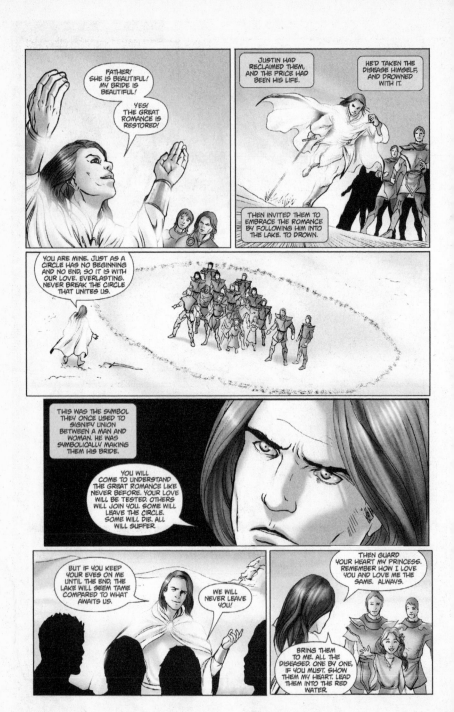

TED DEKKER is the *New York Times* best-selling author of more than twenty novels. He is known for stories that combine adrenaline-laced plots with incredible confrontations between good and evil. He lives in Texas with his wife and children.

For the latest news about *Green*, be sure to visit www.TedDekker.com/Green